Haunted Castles of the World

Also by Charles A. Coulombe

Haunted Places in America
Classic Horror Stories

HAUNTED CASTLES OF THE WORLD

Ghostly Legends and Phenomena from Keeps and Fortresses Around the Globe

CHARLES A. COULOMBE

THE LYONS PRESS
Guilford, Connecticut

An imprint of The Globe Pequot Press

To
Tequila Mockingbird
With whom I have plumbed
many of Hollywood's secrets
and lived to tell the tale!

Contents

Acknowledgments

I n a book of this sort, it is hard to thank by name everyone who helped me with it. But some definite thanks must go to Jake Elwell, my long-suffering agent; to Holly Rubino, my editrix at Lyons; to Stephan Baron von Hoeller-Bertram, for long chats with good booze over the topic; to my cousins Ashley and John Barrett and my friend Ben Gribbon for enduring the slings and arrows of outrageous hauntings; to my father, the late Guy J. C. Coulombe, for nurturing both my Catholic Faith and my interest in the weird; and lastly, to the incredible Criswell, who by his mere presence made my childhood. . . er. . . memorable.

Introduction

Ever since the Globe Theatre first performed Shakespeare's *Hamlet* back in the seventeenth century, ghosts and castles have been inseparable in the popular mind. When the ghost of Hamlet's father took his immortal stroll along the battlements at Elsinore, he walked right into the world's imagination. In the medieval world, of which the Bard of Avon was arguably the last literary flower (in English), the existence of ghosts was taken for granted. Whether souls returned from purgatory to right wrongs or have Masses said for them, or the damned bemoaned their fate, or demons masqueraded as the dead in order to gain company, few mortals doubted that the dead could (and did) walk, if God so allowed it.

In this, the Catholics of the Middle Ages were much like their contemporaries of all religions scattered across the globe: Whatever a given theology's explanation of the occurrence, almost no one denied the fact. But with the Enlightenment's focus on the material world, the age-old belief in ghosts waned among many of the European intelligentsia. Supernatural events were left out or removed from "mainstream" fiction. The tide soon turned again when the new genre of the "gothic" novel often placed its horrors squarely in keeps and palaces; the first of the genre, Horace Walpole's *Castle of Otranto*, firmly holed up its spirits behind fortress walls. This move was echoed by the nineteenth-century Romantics.

Yet the juxtaposition of the risen dead with the castles and palaces of royalty and nobility was not confined to literature—far from it. Humanity's fascination with the highborn is as old as its fascination with ghosts. There are reasons for this, of course. In Old Europe, as in all other pre-modern societies, most common folk were farmers. Concerned with their day-to-day survival, they led lives of incredible toil (outside of the numerous feast days). But their lords, apart from making life-and-death decisions for the entire community (itself a reason to be interested in their doings), spent their time in more glamorous pursuits: hunting, fighting, and the rigors of courtly love. Larger than life (at least to their subjects), such people's days were filled with exciting episodes.

This being true while the old duke was alive, how much truer after his death? While a peasant might come back to haunt his hovel, this sort of event was not nearly so compelling to village storytellers as the old duke's return to the blue room of his castle on the anniversary of his death! The fact that said death was perhaps bound up with a major historical event—or at least, some scandal—added to the interest. It might also be an oblique reference to justice, which is so often eluded in life, being at last meted out beyond the grave.

Of course, the standing of royalty and nobility fell greatly, thanks to the revolutions which rocked the Earth during the course of the eighteenth, nineteenth, and twentieth centuries. These in turn arose from that very Enlightenment which had so damaged the belief in ghosts. But in neither case was the victory of "modernity" complete.

One reason for this is psychological: Men fear, and men revere. The darkness always frightens us, and the titled always fascinate us, as such popular magazines as *People, Hello!, and Point de Vue* remind the reader. So powerful is this latter instinct that it survives in republics, such as the United States, where kings and earls are no more. As C. S. Lewis put it, "Where men are forbidden to honor a king they honor millionaires, athletes, or film stars instead: even famous prostitutes or gangsters." So it is in our own country, and, not surprisingly, that such folk in America are often the topic of ghost stories after they have departed from this world.

Their doings help dispel the boredom of modern life, where the average American works 155 days a year to pay his income tax, rather than his medieval ancestor's 30 days' hard labor for his feudal lord. As with our ancestors, the lives and deaths of the rich and famous continue to attract our attention. This is doubtless why we thrill to hear of Marilyn Monroe's haunting of a mirror at the Hotel Roosevelt in Hollywood, or the mysterious "Lady in Black's" annual pilgrimage to Valentino's grave.

The other reason we still pay attention is that such hauntings continue—or, at least, people continue to report them. Revolutions may come and go, crowns rise and fall, but Lady Catherine Howard still walks the haunted corridor at Hampton Court Palace. Few of the living, indeed, who traverse that spot (this author included) may hear or see anything untoward—but a favored few do.

Moreover, as noted, the haunted castles and palaces of renown have witnessed amazing historical events. We should not be surprised if Henry VIII, his hands bloodied by thousands of victims, returns to Windsor; nor that the gentle shade of Mary Queen of Scots occasionally appears at various locations immortalized by the episodes of her tragic life.

One of the requirements of Greek tragedy was that its doomed protagonists be great kings or nobles of honored families. Certainly, many an aristocratic line has suffered more than its share of evil fortune. Why should it come as a surprise that such events are spawners of ghosts, or that such spirits might return to their former homes?

We will look at a few such places around the world. While most of our chosen spots will be castles or palaces in the accepted sense, a few are not. In the British Commonwealth, our featured haunts are (or were) residences of the local representatives of the monarchy—often noble themselves. In the United States, our castles will simply be the residences of the wealthy. Consciously modeled on the castles of Europe, these American châteaus were generally built by people who, due to their fortune and social standing, would have been made nobles had they lived in monarchies. As a rule, castles or palaces still lived in—rather than those turned into museums—will be favored, although the latter group is also represented. There is a special thrill in hearing about a haunting from the ghost's descendant!

Whether you are going to view these places in person, or stay home with the doors and windows locked and all the lights turned on, you will certainly have a turn or two. The author hopes that your tour is entertaining. But you may end by wondering what sort of ghosts our modern, untitled leadership shall leave behind in their condos to frighten future generations.

Charles A. Coulombe
Arcadia, California
Lammas Eve, 2004

Haunted Castles of the World

If England Were
What England Seems

Although the United States have been independent since 1783 (and only the thirteen easternmost states were settled by the British), England continues to maintain her hold on the American mind. A large part of this, of course, is due to the English language. The legacies of Chaucer, Shakespeare, and the rest form as much a part of the American literary background as they do the British.

To this psychological and linguistic tie must be added an institutional one. The thirty-seven states not founded by the British were nevertheless modeled after those that were. The whole panoply of government—bicameral legislatures, governors, counties, sheriffs, notaries, courts, judges, mayors, all of it—was adapted lock, stock, and warrant from the officers of the Crown.

With these imports came also a taste for the uncanny. The strange English folklore of ghosts, witches, and sundry other odd things made the jump across the Atlantic alongside government and literature. The English have always been a people in love with the uncanny. There are few towns in England that do not boast a bevy of spirits raised from the dead—to warn, to punish, to frighten, or simply to remind. This spectral company makes itself at home in old abbeys, in churches, in manor houses, and even in council flats. But it is in the castles and palaces of the wealthy and renowned that they are most reliably to be found.

"The government of England is as stormy as the seas that surround her," runs an old French proverb. Though it may no longer be true today, the number of civil wars, insurrections, and royal overthrows that dot the English past are astonishing. They have left their mark on the countryside, to be sure; but more telling still are those elements of that bloody past that return—by night or otherwise.

But in addition to the ghosts of kings and nobles undone by politics, there are other signs of the supernatural. Some great families have ghostly animals or people, which appear when a relative is going to die. Other apparitions seem to appear for no reason at all. There are even species of weird figures—like the Black Dog. A figure seen in various locales from Dartmoor to Northumberland, this frightening hound, larger than a normal dog and possessed of glowing red eyes, has frightened travelers by night for centuries. Such ghostly canines have even appeared to descendants of the English colonists in Connecticut and the Appalachians. The readers of Sir Arthur Conan Doyle's *The Hound of the Baskervilles* will be familiar with a literary treatment of the occurrence.

It was in England, to be sure, that the modern practice of ghost hunting got its start. Starting about 1860, the country was caught up in a flood of Spiritualism: table-tapping, séances, and planchettes (forerunners of the notorious Ouija board) became the rage in many circles. After two decades of more or less amateur study (to say nothing of a good deal of fraud), the Society for Psychical Research was founded by Cambridge scholars such as Frederic Myers, Professor Sidgwick, and Mr. Gurney. They founded it in an attempt to make rational study of the whole haunting phenomena.

Both the monarchy and the nobility have lost a lot of ground in terms of earthly power in Great Britain since World War I; in 1999, even the right of hereditary peers to sit in the House of Lords was abolished. Many aristocratic families have had to vacate the great houses their ancestors had dwelt in for centuries, leaving them either to such public organizations as the National Trust, or to be made into schools and the like. But while the living members of such clans may have to leave, the dead remain. However much the government of the day may chisel away at the "royal prerogative," King Henry VIII still walks at Windsor—oblivious, presumably, to those who may "serve" his descendants at 10 Downing Street. In the realm of the undead, democracy apparently means little. Those noblemen who cling to their castles, generally by opening them up to the public as part of the "stately home" trade, gleefully treasure whatever tales of haunting they may have inherited with their ancestral estates. These in turn help lure tourists to preserve family ownership—an endeavor the ghosts in question would surely approve of.

At any rate, here are a very few samples of these haunted English homes. It is an old adage of English law that "An Englishman's home is his castle." Apparently this mandate extends beyond the grave!

In the Tower of London
Large as Life

Our first stop is the traditional center of English kings—the Tower of London. Symbol of the sovereignty of the monarch, repository of the crown jewels, its daily and monthly schedules are filled with ceremonies retained from the realm's storied past. The place has an eerie reputation, to be sure; Boris Karloff and Vincent Price's film, *Tower of London,* evokes chills just by mentioning the title. Back in 1934, the songwriting team of R. P. Weston and Bert Lee produced a comic ditty entitled "With Her Head Tucked Underneath Her Arm." Although sung for laughs, it does reveal a common belief that the ghost of a decapitated Anne Boleyn walks within the Tower.

As with its historic foundations, the Tower's reputation for supernatural events stretches back into the remote past. Celtic legend maintains that the White Hill (from which the White Tower, the oldest existing structure at the Tower, derives its name) was the burial site of the head of Bran the Blessed, a king and demigod of old. So long as his cranium rested there, the bards claimed, Britain would be safe from foreign invasion. However, the story went, King Arthur, trusting to his own strength of arms, removed the skull from its resting place, paving the way for the overrunning of Britain by the Saxons.

Whatever truth there may or may not be to that tale, the site of the Tower comes first to prominence after 1066, when William the Conqueror subjected the Saxons in their turn. To hold London, the new ruler built the White Tower in 1078 on the old Roman walls, once a corner of Londinium. Finished in 1097, it towered ninety feet over the surrounding town. Since that time, successive monarchs have added about twenty towers, and many other attendant buildings. The end in sight was to build an impregnable stronghold of royal prestige.

This was accomplished, to be sure. But as with all governments, to maintain their position, the kings of old had to wield power as well. Impressive ceremonies and surroundings were not enough; thus, many of the towers formerly boasted prison cells. In the crypt of the White Tower, torture chambers lurked. Outside, Tower Green hosted executions of royal prisoners, while the hoi polloi were relegated to Tower Hill. But palace, prison, and treasure repository did not exhaust the Tower's uses; it has also served as an observatory, a menagerie, an armory, and now, a museum.

For ghostly purposes, however, it is the Tower's role as a place of execution that has given the place both its frightening reputation and its large crew of spirits. Rival heirs to the throne have met their ends here, as have traitors, con men, and even saints. Down through the centuries, some have come back. Perhaps the earliest recorded was the martyred Saint Thomas à Becket. His ghost first appeared during the thirteenth century, when the Traitor's Gate was being built. A priest, who saw him strike the gate with a crucifix, causing it to collapse, was the witness.

Generations of the various guardians of the Tower have had to deal with its otherworldly inhabitants as part of their job. An event on the night of January 3, 1804, showed that even All the King's Men could not keep out the uncanny. One Corporal Jones saw a woman in a red-patterned white dress coming toward him from the park. As she came up to him, the corporal realized that not only was the pattern blood, but the woman in question was headless. After standing in front of him for about two minutes, she turned about and returned into the park, only to be lost to sight among the by-now falling snow. Further inquiry turned up the fact that a guardsman back in 1784 had murdered his wife and cut off her head, throwing both into the canal at the other end of the park. While the body was recovered, the skull was not; the sentries supposed said wife was coming back to ask for it to be found by the living.

In January 1815 a sentry guarding the Martin Tower saw a spectral bear exiting the Jewel Room. The guard bayoneted the figure, but his weapon passed through the apparition, and although it was embedded in a door, the bear vanished. Perhaps the spirit was a holdover from the zoo of the Tudor kings. In any case, another sentry had observed the proceedings, and backed up the tale. Although the young man died a few days later, (presumably of shock), he told his tale to Edmund Lenthal Swifte, keeper of the crown jewels.

But the ghostly bear (or another like it) was not finished with the garrison of the Tower. In 1864, another soldier saw a ghostly brown bear and tried to bayonet him. As his weapon passed through the phantom animal, the sentry fainted, which action resulted in a court-martial for dereliction of duty. But the charges against the soldier were dropped when two witnesses backed him up. Unlike his hapless comrade of forty-nine years before, this soldier made off with both life and sanity intact.

Keeper Swifte was to have his own encounter with the supernatural two years after the aforementioned bear incident. While dining with his family in their room in the same Martin Tower, Swifte was horrified when his wife screamed. He jumped up, only to see a weird cylinder-shaped apparition, like a glass tube, filled with blue fluid that bubbled. This. . . thing. . . slipped behind Mrs. Swifte, still sitting at the dinner table. After his wife shouted that it was trying to grab her, Swifte threw a chair at the vision. The piece of furniture passed right through it, and the cylinder retreated and disappeared.

While the Martin Tower has its (usually) unseen and baffling tenants, the well-named Bloody Tower hauntings are more easily comprehended. It was here that the two sons of King Edward IV, Edward, Prince of Wales, and Richard, Duke of York, are held in the popular imagination to have been murdered in 1483 by the command of their uncle, Richard, Duke of Gloucester. He was crowned Richard III that year, only to be defeated and killed at the battle of Bosworth Field by the forces of Henry Tudor (later, Henry VII and father of the infamous Henry VIII).

To be fair, Richard's defenders point out that the lads were no threat to him, as Parliament had declared them illegitimate; they adduce evidence that the brothers actually outlived their uncle, perhaps to be put to death by Henry VII himself. Whether or not that is true, starting in the late fifteenth century guards passing the stair in the Bloody Tower saw two small shadows gliding down toward them; it was assumed that these must be the two princes. When, in 1674, workmen found a chest containing skeletons of two young children, the presumption was that they were in fact the princes. While the pathetic little bodies were given royal funerals, modern-day Ricardians point out that only DNA typing could tell us for sure. In any case, it is said that two little ghosts in white shifts, walking hand in hand, still haunt the Bloody Tower, though others claim the funerals put them to rest.

As might be assumed from the quoted song, Anne Boleyn is the best-known spirit said to haunt the Tower. A strange woman, suspected of practicing witchcraft and bearing six fingers on one hand, she was the cause of both Henry VIII's abuse of his queen, Catherine of Aragon, and of his break from the Catholic Church (as well as his murder of hundreds who opposed him). But she was in turn undone by the king's wandering eye, even as Catherine had been. But where the queen lived a blameless life (and was so rendered immune to her ex's thirst for blood), Anne found other male charms more alluring than those of her corpulent paramour.

Executed on Tower Green in 1536, her headless body was interred in an arrow case under the floor of the Chapel Royal of St. Peter ad Vincula (where she shares space with Saint Thomas More, whom she was indirectly responsible for having executed). Not surprisingly, she haunts both chapel and green; but she also makes appearances in the corridors of the White Tower and at the King's House, residence of the governor of the Tower. This latter place is where she was imprisoned before her execution, and where she is usually seen walking on May 19, the anniversary of her death. She will also glide from the King's House to the Chapel Royal of St. Peter ad Vincula; once there, Anne moves down the aisle to her grave under the altar.

Like the bear at Martin Tower, the hapless Anne has also had a bayonet thrust through her, this time by a sentry who challenged her in 1864. Although the doughty soldier did not allow his thrust to be parried by the fact that the target was headless, her incorporeality was too much for him, and he fainted. Facing court-martial for being asleep at his post, other guards exonerated him by repeating their own similar experiences under oath. Nor is it only the enlisted who have enjoyed the beheaded would-be queen's company: a captain of the guard and a sentry saw a light shining from the locked and empty Chapel Royal in the White Tower. Climbing a ladder to look down into the chapel, they saw a procession of people in archaic clothes, led by a headed Anne Boleyn—this last fact allowed the captain to identify her from pictures.

In times past, when executions were still held at the Tower, Anne would also act as a sort of harbinger the night before someone was to share her fate. On one such occasion during World War I, a sergeant of the Artist's Rifles (on duty the night before several spies—including the notorious Carl Lody—were due to be executed) saw Anne in silk dress and white ruff, literally with "her head tucked underneath her arm."

Anne is not the only one of Henry's concubines to take up permanent residence at the Tower. His fifth wife, Catherine Howard, convicted by him of adultery, was sentenced to death alongside her supposed lovers. But she ran from the axman, screaming for Henry's mercy. As always, this was in short supply: The executioner grabbed her and hacked off her head. Now her screams for help are heard in the corridor in front of the room where she was kept before her demise.

On Tower Green, the aged Margaret Pole, Countess of Salisbury (whose son was to be the last Catholic archbishop of Canterbury, and whose family had a better claim to the throne than did Henry VIII), was beheaded for treason in 1541. But the headsman made a bungle of it: Struck by a glancing blow with an ax, Lady Salisbury (in emulation of Catherine Howard) hopped up and attempted to escape. The executioner chased her about, slashing her from behind with his blade, until she expired. The whole unappetizing scene has been reenacted by the ghosts any number of times for hapless sentries.

At the Salt Tower, Lady Jane Grey, duped into attempting to usurp the throne for nine days and executed for her pains, has been seen on the anniversary of her death, February 12, 1554—most notably by two guardsmen in 1957. Her husband, Guilford Dudley (who was killed with her), cries for them both in Beauchamp Tower. The earl of Northumberland, executed the previous year, is also seen from time to time, while the screams of Guy Fawkes under torture are heard in this tower as well.

As recently as 1983 and 1985, two different guards saw Sir Walter Raleigh walking about at Byward Tower, where Raleigh had spent his fairly pleasant imprisonment prior to being executed. Apparently, Sir Walter, looking quite solid, glanced into the guard-room for a short while and then vanished.

These are only a few of the ghostly "delights" (if that is the word) awaiting the hapless visitor at the Tower; for on the grounds, ghostly funeral carriages have been seen, while a spectral squad of soldiers marches there from time to time. Could it be made up of the seemingly endless supply of guards who have seen supernatural events at the Tower? Given the vast number of deaths at the Tower, it is not surprising that guards occasionally spy a phantom garbed in mourning dress; possibly more surprising is the black and empty void that serves her instead of a face.

Yet, in addition to all of this activity, the Tower of London retains its role as totemic guardian of the queen's realm. Bran's head may have long ago been dug up, but the ravens remain. These black birds, time out of mind, have been held to carry the Crown of England's security on their wings. If ever the Tower loses its ravens, runs the legend, the monarchy—and perhaps the nation—will collapse. There may be no truth to the saying, but to avoid taking chances, the birds' wings are clipped and a raven master carefully monitors them.

If one day, despite all these avian efforts, the Crown should fall, one fears the fate in store for any future English president fool-hardy enough to spend the night with the Tower's collection of royal specters.

Her Majesty's Tower of London
London EC3N 4AB
England

Tel: +44 (0) 8707 566060
http://www.hrp.org.uk/webcode/tower_home.asp

Where Our Last King Lingers

Another of William the Conqueror's constructions was Windsor Castle. As with the Tower of London, almost a millennium of royal residence has turned Windsor Castle into an incredible repository of national identity. Located in what were once the wilds of Berkshire and surrounded by Windsor Forest, the castle is the largest and oldest continuously occupied such place in the world. As the queen's favorite residence, it also continues to fulfill its role as an out-of-town escape for the royal family.

One wonders if Her Majesty has ever encountered, as several of her still-living relations are said to have done, the shade of her namesake, Elizabeth I. Apparently, the sound of her high heels tapping on bare floorboards—regardless of whether the room is carpeted or not—is heard. Then, she appears and passes through the library wall into a blocked-up inner room. The first recorded example of this apparition occurred in 1897, when a Guards lieutenant named Carr Glynn encountered the "Virgin Queen." Other witnesses have included Princess Victoria, daughter of the queen of that name, later to be the wife of German kaiser, Friedrich III, and mother to Kaiser Wilhelm II.

Another permanent resident of the library, although completely invisible, is a disembodied voice that asks the question, "What? What? What?" Given the phraseology, it is believed that this query is launched by none other than George III, famous to Americans as our last king. After battling recurring bouts of porphyria, an organic disease that mimics madness, he succumbed to it completely in the last decade of his life. He was often confined to his bedroom, beneath which his guards would march every morning. Despite his affliction, he would pull himself together, returning their salute smartly. After the king's death—while the king's corpse lay in state—the lieutenant commanding the morning patrol looked up to the window and saw His Majesty in his usual place. Astonished, he nevertheless ordered, "Eyes right!" The phantom sovereign gravely saluted in return. To this day, he is said to occasionally be seen sadly looking through the window.

George III lost the Crown of America, as well as his sanity—but at least his death was peaceful. However, his predecessor, Charles I, who fought and lost a bloody civil war, ended up being executed by a vengeful Parliament in 1649. His courage in adversity, his refusal to save his own life by renouncing the institution of bishops, and his exemplary personal piety led the Church of England to canonize him after his son returned to power in 1660 (the only time that institution has claimed to make a saint). But holy or not, he has been seen haunting the canon's house in the precincts of the castle's St. George's Chapel, where he was imprisoned by Oliver Cromwell for a time.

In the nearby deanery of the chapel, a less famous but nevertheless angry phantom little boy shouts, "I don't want to go riding today," after which disembodied footsteps stalk off. Another auditory show is put on by the shade of Henry VIII in the deanery cloisters. Groaning in torment, the king who was responsible for creating so many ghosts on his own perhaps receives a bit of otherworldly justice. At the Horseshoe Cloisters, a man leads a horse through the wall. Since the cloisters were once the cavalry stables, this is not too surprising.

The grounds are seemingly as haunted as the castle and its outbuildings. In April of 1906, a sentry from the Coldstream Guards was patrolling the East Terrace when he saw a group of men descending the steps. Challenging them and receiving neither an answer nor compliance with his order to halt, he opened fire. Apart from slightly hesitating as the bullets passed through his form, the lead figure paid no mind to him. At this, the young sentry charged the group, whereupon they vanished. Reporting the event to his superiors, who thoroughly searched the grounds and found nothing, he was confined to barracks for three days as punishment. Presumably, if he ever had any similar experiences thereafter, he kept them to himself.

Guard duty at the castle can be a weary and lonely business. Sentries posted to the Long Walk often think they see the standing stones there moving in the moonlight. Whether or not that is so, in 1926, a young grenadier guard shot himself while on duty. A few weeks later, another grenadier guard, one Sergeant Leake, found himself posted to the same spot. Toward the end of his shift, as he marched back toward the guard box, he saw what he thought was another guardsman. But the face under the bearskin was that of the young suicide. When the relief guard came marching into view, the spirit vanished. Leake found out from the guard he himself had replaced that his predecessor had also seen the dead guard.

It is in the depths of wild Windsor Forest that the most famous ghost may be found—Herne the Hunter. He is so renowned that he found his way into Shakespeare's *Merry Wives of Windsor,* where Sir John Falstaff declares that:

> There is an old tale goes that Herne the Hunter,
> Sometime a keeper here in Windsor Forest,
> Doth all the wintertime, at still midnight,
> Walk round about an oak, with great ragg'd horns.

Of course, this story hearkens back to the medieval kings, when Windsor Forest was a wilderness, whose deer constantly lured royal hunters into its depths. Richard II's favorite huntsman was one Herne, who saved the king's life when a stag that had been brought to earth tried to gore him with his antlers. Although successful in saving his employer's life, Herne himself was seriously wounded. A local wise woman nursed him back to health, but part of the cure was that Herne must wear a hood with stag's antlers. This odd headgear did nothing to lessen the king's affection for him, an affection that soon led to tremendous jealousy on the part of other huntsmen. These men in turn framed him for theft, which led to a loss of the king's favor. Shamed and saddened by this turn of events, Herne hanged himself on a tree, ever after called "Herne's Oak," in what is now the Home Park.

But that was far from the end of Herne the Hunter. He cursed the men who had pushed him to suicide. He continued to ride the forest after his death, and one by one they joined him in a proverbial "wild hunt." Through the forest of Windsor they rode, and ride still, if locals can be believed. For whenever England is threatened, Herne and his unwilling companions prowl. Two young lads from nearby Eton College encountered them on the eve of Edward VIII's abdication in 1936, and even some of today's royals are said to have seen or heard them. So if you ever think about taking a stroll through the woods at Windsor by night, let us hope, for England's sake, that you do not!

Ticket Sales and Information Office
The Official Residences of The Queen
London SW1A 1AA
England

Tel: +44 (0) 2077 667304
Fax: +44 (0) 2079 309625
http://www.royal.gov.uk/output/page557.asp
http://www.thecrownestate.co.uk/65_the_windsor_estate_04_02_07
E-mail: bookinginfo@royalcollection.org.uk

A Gallery Haunted

Although relatively new (at a mere four and a half centuries old), the suburban County of Surrey, Hampton Court has in its lifetime lived through four identities. Built in 1525 by Cardinal Wolseley, it was taken over in short order by Henry VIII, who never saw a bit of Church property he could resist. He renovated the place considerably, and it remained an active royal palace until 1760. As George III preferred Windsor, Hampton Court was eventually divided into "grace and favor" apartments, where those who had served the crown faithfully were allowed to live for free. In recent decades it has been transformed into a museum, although it has always retained an official standing as a palace.

As might be expected, its ghostly heritage centers around Henry VIII's time, although virtually all ages of the palace are covered by the over thirty apparitions recorded there at various times. Henry's third wife, Jane Seymour, died at Hampton Court giving birth to Edward VI (under whom the *Book of Common*

Prayer was promulgated and the Mass outlawed); her ghost walks through one of the palace's courtyards carrying a candle.

Edward, in his turn, had a nurse named Sibell Penn. She outlived her young charge, being buried in the palace grounds in 1562. When, in 1829, building work disturbed her tomb, a strange whirring noise was heard in the southwest wing of Hampton Court. Tracing the noise to a brick wall, the workmen discovered a small forgotten room. In it was an old spinning wheel, just like Sibell's. She also put in an appearance in the bedroom of one of the "grace and favor" apartments. The female tenant awoke one night to find a woman bent over and staring at her. Demanding to know what the visitor wanted, she received the reply that the apparition needed a home. The unflappable tenant responded in no uncertain terms that she herself owned the bedroom and there was no room for another, whereupon the visitor vanished. Nevertheless, Sibell has continued her visits to Hampton Court through the present day, especially in Tennis Court Lane.

The best-known ghost at Hampton Court is Henry's fifth wife, Catherine Howard, whom we met screaming for mercy at the Tower. In contrast to her purely auditory performance at the Tower, at Hampton Court she is repeatedly seen, dressed in white, her face distorted by fear, running down one of the galleries ever after called the "Haunted Gallery" in her honor. She does scream at Hampton Court as well, though. This activity is by way of repeating an action that Catherine performed in 1541. Accused of adultery, she was at Hampton Court under house arrest. She was once able to break free of her guards. Running forty feet down the hall, she banged on the door of Henry's private chapel, begging hysterically for mercy. She would receive no more at this time than she did later at the Tower, and was dragged back to her room to await transport to the Tower a few days later.

The ill-starred queen has made herself known in ways other than the reenactment. Many have seen the ringed hand of a woman knocking on a door in the interior of the palace. One witness sketched the ring; it matched one worn by Catherine in a portrait. In April 2000, two women on two separate guided tours felt that something invisible had punched them. They fainted outside the door to Henry VIII's private chapel, and described feeling hot and sweaty upon revival.

At this, the palace authorities decided enough was enough. Sightings and hearings are one thing, but physical damage is another. They consulted a psychologist, one Dr. Richard Wiseman. Dr. Wiseman went to work, conducting a four-night vigil at the palace. Among his equipment were video cameras, pressure gauges, electromagnetic sensors, humidity monitors, and a thermal imaging camera. Although over half of four hundred Hampton Court visitors declared that they could feel a "presence" in the haunted gallery, and claimed they felt also a sudden drop in temperature, few said that they actually saw Elizabethan figures. Wiseman's findings were inconclusive.

While the unique ventilation of the palace may account for many if not all of the cold spots, more, and even stranger occurrences, were in store for Hampton Court Palace. On December 19, 2003, the Associated Press reported that the closed-circuit television cameras at the palace had picked up what appeared to be a ghost. When asked by reporters if the whole report was a hoax, Vikki Wood, a Hampton Court spokeswoman, declared that security guards had spotted the figure in closed-circuit television footage that they had checked to see who was leaving open one of the palace's fire doors. "In the still photograph, the figure of a man in a robe-like garment is shown stepping from the shadowy doorway, one arm reaching out for the door handle. The area around the man is somewhat blurred, and his face appears unnaturally white compared with his outstretched hand," the AP report continued. Palace security guard James Faukes said, "It was incredibly spooky because the face just didn't look human."

Is the figure perhaps Cardinal Wolseley, displeased with what succeeding occupants have done to his palace? No one knows for sure—but when walking the Haunted Gallery, do be careful. Hampton Court does not need another permanent tenant, "grace and favor" or otherwise!

Hampton Court Palace
East Molesey
Surrey KT8 9AU
England

Tel: +44 (0) 8707 527777
http://www.hrp.org.uk/webcode/hampton_home.asp

The Earl Marshal's Domain

Arundel Castle is the second-largest castle in Great Britain. This is fitting, because the Howards, dukes of Norfolk, are the premier nobility in the realm, second only to the royal family in precedence. His Grace the Duke is Earl Marshal of England; in earlier times, that meant he commanded the sovereign's troops. Today, his role is strictly ceremonial—but that means a great deal in England. To begin with, as hereditary earl marshal, the duke is chief of the College of Arms, the heraldic body which designs and registers coats of arms for individuals, public bodies, and governments across the English-speaking world. He also organizes many of the British Crown's ceremonies: the June procession and service for the Order of the Garter at Windsor; the state opening of Parliament, most often in November; state funerals; and the sovereign's coronation at Westminster, to name just a few.

Thus the current duke, like so many of his ancestors, is at the center of the British establishment. The irony in this is that he is also a Catholic, and thus may never sit upon the throne he serves so diligently. This dichotomy, which dates back to the Reformation, has in large part determined the history of the Howard family. So too has their possession of Arundel itself. On a visit there in 1992, this writer noticed that the estate workers all referred to His Grace as "our Duke." Not a bad testimony to his character.

Of course, the Howards have not always been at Arundel. Built on an existing Saxon fortification, the site was given by William the Conqueror to Roger de Montgomery in 1067. His task was to defend the southern coast and the river Arun from invasion by foreigners. The following year he began Arundel. Remnants of that first castle survive alongside architecture from every period up to and including the Victorian. Similarly, Arundel's armory contains weapons from the fifteenth to the eighteenth century, and interior furnishings to match. In the Fitzalan Chapel, built in early English Gothic style in 1380, the earls of Arundel and dukes of Norfolk rest in a "fine series of tombs." Although de Montgomery's son was banished for treason in 1105, in 1138 Arundel was granted again to the d'Albini family. It has in turn passed down through the female line to the Fitzalans, and then the Howards.

Many members of this family have been remarkable. They took firm—often losing—sides in the battles of their time; hence their adhesion to the Catholic faith when Henry VIII and Elizabeth I were making it hard to do that. This led to many bizarre and romantic escapades, and, as we know, such are perfect for haunting! When one of the Howards is about to die, for example, a white owl is always observed flying around the windows.

Arundel boasts a number of regular guests from the spirit world. The first, to be found in the old keep—the ancient tower around which all else grew—is old Roger de Montgomery, to whom William the Conqueror gave Arundel in the first place. People encounter him there from time to time, presumably keeping watch over his old. . . er. . . haunt.

There is also a young woman, dressed in white, who walks the Hiorne Tower in the grounds. Located behind the castle, in Arundel Park, the structure was designed in the eighteenth century by the noted architect, Francis Hiorne. Apparently, in life, the young lady had leapt to her death, distraught over a love affair. She appears on moonlit nights, much to the discomfiture of the groundskeepers.

In the library, renowned as one of the finest Gothic rooms in the country, a man is occasionally seen looking through the books. What makes him unusual is the fact that he appears to be a vibrant shade of blue, and has been seen doing his browsing since 1630. The Blue Man floats as much as he walks, and was apparently the inspiration for the ghost Gabriel, who haunted Lord Peter Wimsey's ancestral home in Dorothy Sayers's *Busman's Holiday.*

In addition to an unnamed cavalier, Arundel is also home to a kitchen boy who lived two centuries ago, and helped out in the scullery. Beaten to death for some minor offense, he is seen in his old workplace, scrubbing away at pots and pans.

There is another ghost who occasionally puts in an appearance in the servants' quarters. One night in 1958, a trainee footman went to turn off the drawbridge lights at 11:00 P.M. As he walked down the ground-floor corridor to reach the switchbox, he noticed something odd. He saw the head and shoulders of a man with long hair wearing a light gray tunic with loose sleeves. The footman said, "The image was like that of an old photo, with the outline blurred. Because of poor light I could see nothing below waist level. As I walked on, the strong impression seemed to fade and he had gone."

As much a part of the country's history as any royal palace, Arundel awaits your visit. But be warned: You may run into a very alive bit of England's past!

Arundel Castle
Arundel
West Sussex BN18 9AB
England

Tel: +44 (0) 1903 882173
Fax: +44 (0) 1903 884581
http://www.arundelcastle.org/
E-mail: info@arundelcastle.org

A Grisly Family Heirloom

A far cry from the great palaces and castles of royalty and high nobility are the manor houses of the gentry. But they are still grand by our standards. Moreover, it is a curious fact that while few English noble titles date back to the Middle Ages, many families of the "squirearchy" have remained in their own locations since then. A typical example is the family that has dwelt at Burton Agnes Hall, in Yorkshire, since 1173.

In that year, Roger de Stuteville built a Norman manor house on the property. One of his daughters was named Agnes, and it is believed that de Stuteville named his property in his daughter's honor. The original house comprises a lower chamber in the original Norman style, and an upper room, built as a great hall by Sir Walter Griffith (whose family had inherited the place from a de Stuteville heiress) in the mid-fifteenth century—complete with thatched roof. A seventeenth-century brick shell, added when the old house was being used as a laundry, conceals all of this antiquity.

This structure is now under the guardianship of the government organization English Heritage, the "new" house having superseded the original manor house.

In 1599, Sir Henry Griffith had already begun the erection of a new family home in the Midlands, closer to the center of action at the court than the remote old family home. But in that year, he was appointed to the Council of the North. He abandoned his building plans, and instead started construction of a new home near the old one at Burton Agnes. Sir Henry hired Robert Smithson, master mason to Elizabeth I (and responsible for such other famous houses as Longleat, Wollaton, and Hardwick), as architect.

The result was a jewel of Elizabethan architecture, albeit with Palladian and Victorian additions. The gatehouse is similarly noteworthy, while the rooms in the main house are treasuries of English furnishings from more than four centuries. Burton Agnes's gardens are also spectacular. While Sir Henry's work lives on, his name did not, as he had three daughters (whose portraits hang in the inner hall) and no sons. His eldest, Frances, married Sir Matthew Boynton, and the estate remained in the Boynton family until the end of the nineteenth century. The heiress, Cecily Boynton, married Thomas Lamplugh Wickham; as is customary in such cases, he assumed the name and arms of Boynton. Since their eldest son, Major Henry Fairfax Wickham-Boynton, was killed in World War II, Burton Agnes passed to their younger son, Marcus. His daughter, Mary Constance Boynton, has in her turn passed the place to her son, Simon Cunliffe-Lister.

Mother and son continue to watch over the family home. One of their great boasts is the queen's state bedroom. Plaster plant fronds and branches grow around the walls and ceiling, while the chimneypiece, flanked as it is by a pair of Corinthian columns, supports an overmantel divided into three panels by still more columns. It is decorated by the allegorical figures of Patience, Truth, Constance, and Victory, opposed by Tribulation, Fraud,

Danger, and Treason. Not only is it beautiful, but it may also reveal why Burton Agnes has remained in the family since the 1600s, when so many other homes have lost their ancestral owners. It is well documented that this beauty conceals a spooky secret.

Sir Henry's youngest daughter, Katharine Anne (who was always called by her middle name) died in this room in 1620. While the new hall was being built, Anne watched and spoke of it constantly, saying that it was the most beautiful house that could ever be built. As it neared completion, Anne went to visit their neighbors, the Saint Quintins. They then lived at Harpham, about a mile away. But near St. John's Well, Anne was attacked and robbed by a band of criminals. She was brought home so badly hurt that she died a few days later. As she lay dying, she told her sisters that she would never rest unless some part of her remained in "our beautiful home as long as it shall last." Anne forced them to promise that on her death her head would be severed and kept in the hall forever. Hoping to comfort her, the sisters agreed to her eerie request. Of course, they did not mean to keep their word, and so Anne was duly buried in the churchyard.

But Anne returned from the grave, haunting the room where she died and frightening the denizens of the house out of their wits. Eventually, the sisters sought the advice of their local vicar. When told of their promise to Anne, he counseled them to keep their promise. In due course, Anne was disinterred, her skull removed, and brought into the house. Abruptly, her visitations ceased.

As might be expected, succeeding generations were none too pleased with their grisly talisman. From time to time, the skull would be removed. Once it was thrown away; another time, a descendant buried it in the garden. The result was always the same. Pandemonium occurred as Anne returned to her old home, resolved to frighten the miscreants out of their wits. At last, it was decided to place the head in a wall niche in the Great Hall, which was then bricked up. Both sides were happy—Anne, because the promise made to her was kept, and the family, because they did not have to look at her skull.

Enjoy the beauties of Burton Agnes Hall—but just remember that continued tranquility there is based upon a ghostly bargain.

Burton Agnes Hall
Burton Agnes, Driffield
Yorkshire YO25 0ND
England

Tel: +44 (0) 1262 490324
Fax: +44 (0) 1262 490513
http://www.burton-agnes.co.uk/
E-mail: burton.agnes@farmline.com

Muncaster Frights

Muncaster Castle, in the far northern county of Cumbria, has been in the Pennington family since it was built in 1258, a half-century after the land was granted to Alan de Peningtone. In 1464, after his defeat at the Battle of Hexham, the saintly King Henry VI found refuge here at the hands of Sir John Pennington. (Sir John's shepherds had found the king hiding after the debacle.) In return for this hospitality, Henry gave his drinking bowl to his hosts, declaring that "as long as it should remain quite whole and unbroken, the Penningtons would live and thrive in the place." Still intact, the bowl is called the "Luck of Muncaster" today.

In 1783, Sir John Pennington built the tower he named Chapels at the place where the shepherds found the royal fugitive. That same year, he was created First Baron Muncaster in the Irish Peerage. Over the course of the nineteenth century, the house was much embellished by successive Lords Muncaster. In 1917, the fifth and last Lord Muncaster died, and the castle reverted to his mother's family, the Ramsdens. They in turn took the name Pennington. The last heiress, Phyllida Pennington, married Patrick Gordon-Duff (now Gordon-Duff-Pennington), and the couple currently reigns over Muncaster and its ghosts—indeed, it has its share! Friends, family, and visitors alike have seen doors open and shut by themselves, and have heard disembodied footsteps.

Patrick Gordon-Duff-Pennington has said that in wintertime, regardless of the weather, such footsteps follow him in the dark: "I didn't like it one little bit. The dogs didn't like it either. I always thought this house was a fairly normal house, but just lately it has become extremely strange."

Muncaster enjoys at least four known ghostly tenants. One is not a surprise—Henry VI, murdered in the Tower of London after Edward IV's victory at the Battle of Tewkesbury, appears in the chamber he occupied. It is not too surprising, perhaps, that the king might return to a place where he knew the warmth and happiness given by loyal, loving subjects.

A much less pleasant apparition than that of the holy king is a young carpenter, murdered in the late sixteenth century. Having fallen in love with Helwise, the daughter of Sir Ferdinand Pennington, the young man feared his irascible master's wrath. Sir Ferdinand ordered his jester, Thomas Skelton (alias "Tom Fool"), to murder his daughter's would-be swain. This Tom happily did, severing the carpenter's head and bringing it to Sir Ferdinand as proof of the deed. Now the carpenter's headless wraith stalks the battlements of Muncaster. Sometimes, so does Tom Fool.

But murdering the youth was not Tom's only accomplishment. Before his death in 1600, he acquired quite a reputation for unpleasant "tricks." He used to sit under a chestnut tree, still growing just outside the doors of the castle. Wayfarers, if Tom took a disliking to them, would find themselves directed to the quicksand on the shore rather than to the ford and the London road.

Tom's portrait now hangs in one of Muncaster's corridors. He may be seen there in addition to occasional appearances on the battlements. Hanging next to the picture is Tom's will, in which he accurately foretold his own death by drowning—possibly in retribution for the many he had sent to their own demise. A female tourist, while staring at Tom's portrait one day, heard footsteps clattering on the stone flooring coming up behind her. Whirling around, she saw no one. Of course, the fact that the corridor is carpeted rendered the episode even more bizarre.

The most haunted room at Muncaster is the Tapestry Room, located in a little-used wing of the castle. One James Cartland, an archivist and family friend, stayed at Muncaster in the early 1980s. He was put up in the Tapestry Room, and had rather an odd night. Alone in that wing of the castle, he heard a "sort of strange muttering sound, as if someone was talking." After putting his head up the chimney to determine if the noise came from the wind, he found that it was a still night—no wind played through the fireplace. He then walked out into the corridor but again heard nothing. "When I returned to my room, the noise was still going on, and was more audible by then. It was definitely the sound of a child crying. I got back into bed—I never slept a wink that night. It was a terrible night!"

A year earlier, a teenage girl staying in the same room had heard footsteps along the corridor outside. The door of her room opened and the room was filled with the weeping of an invisible child. Charles James Ruthven Howard, the twelfth earl of Carlisle (1923–1994), also faced the weeping child, as he told the curator of the castle at the time, Philip Denham-Cookes: "Lord Carlisle told me that he had only stayed once in Muncaster and that was in the Tapestry Room. He had been woken up during the middle of the night by the sound of a young child weeping. He admitted he had never been more terrified in his life."

From whence comes the crying in the Tapestry Room? According to James Cartland: "[T]he tapestry room had been part of the old nurseries, and. . . those rooms had been altered in some way. And so I immediately thought. . . my goodness. . . those children lived in these rooms. . . they were the nurseries. It's rather unnerving!" But which of the children who lived there is responsible for the haunting? The answer may lie in the death of Lady Margaret Pennington, daughter of Gamel Augustus, the third Baron Muncaster, at age eleven. Screaming fits and wild sobbing preceded her demise. Perhaps they still echo down the years! But all is not gloom, for sometimes a lady is heard singing, as if to comfort a sick child.

Unfortunately, there are also somewhat less pleasant forces at work in the room. The stereotypical cold spots show up, to be sure. Black figures sometimes lean over frightened sleepers in the antique four-poster bed; still others feel a heavy weight dropping on them. Nor is that all. A paranormal investigation team observed a black, featureless figure walking into the Tapestry Room and vanishing. Is this the being that opens the door and so paves the way for the spectral crying?

The grounds at Muncaster are no refuge from the unearthly either, due to the "Muncaster Boggle," or White Lady, who prowls the gardens. She is believed to be the ghost of Mary Bragg, a local woman murdered in 1805. Although not employed at Muncaster (she was a housekeeper at nearby Ravenglass), her life and death were bound up with the staff at the castle. Mary was in love with the castle footman, but so too was one of the maids on the Muncaster payroll.

What this maid's part in the tragedy might have been cannot be determined precisely, but the locals firmly believe that she was conspiring with the two men who showed up at Mary's home one night, maintaining that her lover was ill. Offering to take her to him, they brought Mary to a tree on a lonely road and killed her. She was found weeks later, floating in the nearby river Esk. Due to the amount of damage that feeding eels had done to her head, the coroner was unable to determine the cause of death. Mary Bragg still wanders about Muncaster's grounds, offering an outdoor alternative to the haunting within. Oddly enough, it is said that the tree where locals claim she was murdered bled when it was cut down.

If you are interested, Muncaster does rent out the Tapestry Room at special group rates. But alarms are set, and guests are not released until morning. In any case, although visitors may stay in the Tapestry Room if they like, it would be wise to think about Henry VI, who gave the "Muncaster Luck." Long may it hold!

Muncaster Castle
Ravenglass
Cumbria CA18 1RQ
England

Tel: +44 (0) 1229 717614
http://www.muncaster.co.uk/index.htm
E-mail: info@muncaster.co.uk

Is Chillingham
England's Most Haunted Castle?

Like neighboring Cumbria, Northumberland's history prior to the eighteenth century was the story of the Borders—the debatable land between England and Scotland, filled with raids, banditry, and murder. On both sides of the frontier, landed families built castles to impose order upon chaos (or else to provide strongholds from whence to take advantage of that chaos). One of the most extraordinary to survive on the English side is Chillingham Castle.

Originally built by the Hentercombe family, Chillingham came into the possession of the Grey family of Wark in the thirteenth century. Sir William Grey was created Lord Grey of Wark in 1623. Dying in 1674, he was succeeded by his son, Ford, Lord Grey, who was in turn created first earl of Tankerville. Although he died in 1701 without a male heir, his title passed to Charles Bennet, second Baron Ossulston, who had married his daughter Mary six years earlier.

The earliest parts of the castle date back to thirteenth century, and the north and south fronts of the castle were redesigned in the 1600s by Inigo Jones. In 1828 Sir Jeffry Wyatville designed formal Italianate gardens for the castle. For at least seven hundred years the park surrounding the castle (corralled in 1270) has been home to a herd of wild white cattle, which numbers between forty and sixty. These animals are one of six herds in Great Britain, and are the descendants of the wild cattle that roamed the island freely before the Romans came. Roe and fallow deer share the woods with them.

The Greys lived happily at Chillingham until the death of the ninth earl of Tankerville in 1980, at which time his son, the tenth earl, was forced to sell. Fortunately, the Sir James Knott Charitable Trust purchased the park and woodlands, thereby preserving the future of the herd. An English baronet, Sir Humphry Wakefield, purchased the castle itself. Coming from a family known in Cumbria's Lake District for four centuries, Sir Humphry was sensitive to Chillingham, the more so since his wife, Lady Wakefield, is a descendant of the Greys herself. Thus, certain continuity has been maintained, which the couple's two sons and daughter will doubtless carry on.

The family is happy to show visitors such features as the most ancient room in the castle—the Edward I Room—as well as the James I Drawing Room, the state rooms, the banqueting hall, the minstrels' hall, and the castle library, all of which reflect several prosperous centuries of family history. These form quite a contrast to the medieval torture chamber, with its stretching rack, bed of nails, nailed barrel, spiked chair, Iron Maiden, and sundry thumb screws, chains, leg irons, cages, man traps, and branding irons. There is also the dungeon, lit by a narrow slit in the thick wall, with the graffiti left by former prisoners. This is no Disneyland exhibit: Through the trapdoor in the floor, the actual bones of a child may be seen in the vault below. As mentioned, the history of the Borders was bloody and unpleasant.

With this in mind, it is no shock that Chillingham is a contender for the title of most haunted castle in England. In October 2000, Fox Family Channel, after a contest, dared the Olson family from rural Illinois to spend the night at Chillingham. The result was an extremely frightening broadcast. The five members of the family heard and felt a number of strange things, and their teenage son was the focus of some very unpleasant activity.

The best-known phantom apparently no longer walks. Dubbed the "Blue Boy," or the "Radiant Boy," he formerly haunted the Pink Room, which remains in the family's private apartments. At one time, when the clock from the castle tower struck midnight, the cries and moans of a child in agony and fear were heard. These noises emitted from a spot next to a passage that had been cut through a ten-foot-thick wall into the adjoining tower. As the cries died away, a bright halo of light formed close to an old four-poster bed. Whoever slept in the bed was then approached by the apparition of a young boy dressed in blue, surrounded by the light. Those who saw him declared that he wore clothes from the Restoration era of Charles II.

During restoration work in the 1920s, the wall was opened. Inside were found the bones of a young boy and scraps of a blue dress. Alongside this macabre display was found the skeleton of a man where the fireplace is now situated. This was close to a trapdoor opening to the stone arches of the vaults below. The bones were removed and given a Christian burial in the nearby churchyard, and since then the Blue Boy of Chillingham has not been seen. But all is not completely tranquil in the Pink Room. Personal guests of the family who stay there report strange blue flashes in the middle of the night.

Other ghostly inhabitants include Lady Mary Berkeley, in life the spouse of Ford, Lord Grey of Wark and Chillingham and first earl of Tankerville. Her husband ran off with her own sister, Lady Henrietta. Despite winning the resulting suit, she was left alone with the castle and her baby daughter. Denizens of the castle hear the rustling of her long skirts in the corridors and stairs of Chillingham, accompanied by a rush of cold. Her portrait, which formerly hung in the nursery, was also a site of disturbance. Resident children and their nurse have averred that Lady Mary has stepped out of her frame and followed them around.

In the inner pantry, the Tankervilles' silver was stored, and a footman slept there to guard it. After going to bed one night the footman was asked for water by a very pale lady in white. Supposing her to be a guest, he turned away to get her something to drink, when he remembered that he was locked in, and that no one could have entered. Spinning around, he found that his strange visitor was gone. One guest who recorded her "psychic impressions" in the various rooms of the castle (not having been told of the castle's claimed hauntings) saw the lady in white also. She felt her yearning for water, and that she "must have been slowly poisoned in olden times."

One upper bedroom at Chillingham had long had a reputation for an oppressive atmosphere. A lady's maid assigned this room was discovered the next morning sleeping on the sofa in the dining hall. She had fled the room in a panic, although she could not say why. It developed that a chef had committed suicide in the chamber. As Sir Humphry dryly remarks, "We no longer use it as a bedroom."

Directly underneath this room is the library. Folks reading there often overhear two male voices, but they are not clear, and they immediately stop if one drops his reading or writing to listen to them. Although many have heard them, no one knows why or what they are talking about.

Many more tales are told of these sorts of events. George Montagu Bennet, the seventh earl of Tankerville, married Leonora van Marter. She wrote an account of some of the strange events that overtook her while living at Chillingham in the 1920s.

After having met Lord Bennet (as her future husband was called before succeeding his father as earl) some months before, she had an odd dream. At the time, the future Lady Tankerville did not expect that she would marry him, and knew nothing at all about Chillingham, having never been there or even having it described to her. She was traveling abroad at the time. Waking at sunrise, she found herself walking through a place she would later recognize as the West Lodge entrance leading into the avenue at Chillingham. Yet she knew it was Lord Bennet's home. Since she could not see the castle itself, she wondered if this was an omen that she would never visit it in the flesh. Just then, a young man came up and introduced himself as Lord Bennet's brother, saying, "I have come to walk with you until George is ready." They turned back and walked toward the park, whereupon Lord Bennet arrived and his brother disappeared. Years later, when she first saw the brother's photo, she recognized him as the man from her dream.

Just after midnight, one morning in the spring of 1924, Lady Tankerville was standing at her dressing table brushing her hair. She became aware of the presence of a friend of hers and her husband's, an army officer whom they knew to be very sick, albeit not terminally. He seemed to be gazing at her with curiosity, and looked as if he were about to speak. She thought to throw on a dressing gown, but he disappeared. She told her husband of the event, and of course it turned out the next day that their friend had died at that moment. Lady Tankerville saw many other spirits at the castle during her stay, including a Dominican abbess.

Certainly, successive inhabitants of Chillingham have seen many spirits who walk. Apparently casual visitors do as well. If you find yourself that way, perhaps en route to Scotland, stopping by may be a good way to say farewell to the country—both the living and dead citizens of it.

Chillingham Castle
Chillingham, Alnwick
Northumberland NE66 5NJ
England

Tel: +44 (0) 1668 215359
Fax: +44 (0) 1668 215463
http://www.chillingham-castle.com
E-mail: stay@chillingham–castle.com

In Wild Wales

According to the prophecy of Taliesin, legendary poet and contemporary of King Arthur, the Welsh would not lose their land in the face of invasion. Of course, it proved true. Despite the best efforts of the Britons, they were pushed out of England, and forced into the far west of their lands—to Cumbria, Cornwall, and Wales. Others fled to the "Little Britain over the Sea," which is now modern Brittany. In spite of this wave of newcomers, the Welsh maintained their customs, memories, and beliefs, to be sure.

In addition to the ancient Celtic lore of their ancestors, with its stories of fairies, witches, wizards, and the "second sight"—the gift of prophecy, the ability to see normally invisible things, and, often, the talent for diagnosing illness (all expressed in their own language)—and the earliest versions of the Arthurian legend, the Welsh had and still hold a firm belief in ghosts. There are few Welsh towns that have no haunted spots, no fairy mounds, nor any supernatural harbingers of death. These occasionally have practical value.

In 1890, the residents around Morfa near Port Talbot in Glamorganshire seemed to undergo a virtual siege of phantom funeral processions, ghostly hounds, and various other unearthly visitations, which included vivid dreams warning of disaster. The net result was to frighten many coal miners at the local mine into skipping work one morning. This was just as well, because a subterranean explosion that day claimed the lives of eighty workers who did go to work. Tragedy that it was, the affair would have killed hundreds more had not various oddities warned them off.

But Welsh history is very bloody and exactly the kind of thing to give birth to both castles and ghosts. Although at first the Welsh continued bitter guerrilla warfare against the Saxons from their little country, the better-organized English (as the invaders came to be called) hemmed them in with a wall called Offa's Dyke, during the eighth century. Ultimately, the Welsh's efforts were more damaged in the long run by the great political curse of the Celts: disunity. A number of Welsh principalities emerged, some of which quickly fell victim to the Normans after they in their turn seized England in 1066. Half the country fell under the sway of the "Marcher Lords," Anglo-Norman nobles who established castles to hold the locals under their sway—and many of which now play host to various apparitions. This is not surprising given the turbulent lifestyles of their builders.

In time, however, the Welsh rallied under a native leader, Llywelyn ap Gruffudd, Prince of Wales, who attempted to secure the whole of the country for its inhabitants. But he was defeated and killed in 1282, by the forces of King Edward I. The remaining Welsh leadership offered to cease hostilities if Edward would give them a new prince who was Welsh-born, of spotless character, and who spoke no English. This Edward agreed to. After the Welsh lay down their arms, the wily king named his infant son Prince of

Wales (seeing that he could speak neither English nor anything else), and since that time, the heirs to the throne have been called by that title—as is Prince Charles today. Edward then built a network of mighty castles in the formerly native zone—many of which are haunted today.

But if the principality more or less settled down under English rule (the fifteenth-century revolt of Owen Glendower was an exception), Wales is still a separate country. With its own language and culture, it is unmistakably different from England—as is its attitude toward ghosts!

Where the Prince of Wales
Was Crowned

Caernarfon Castle is an extraordinary sight, as it broods over the picturesque town of the same name. The jewel in the crown of Welsh castles, it is both enormous and in very good repair. Edward I intended it to be the seat of future princes of Wales, and it is in fact the closest thing there is to a royal palace in Wales. The future Edward VIII had his investiture as prince there, as did Charles in 1969. In fact, his investiture was the first ever televised. Broadcast in the United States, the impressive ceremonies and the beautiful castle in which they were staged remain a strong memory for this writer.

The castle site was originally fortified by the Romans in A.D. 80, who called their fort Segontium. After their withdrawal in the late fourth century, it became a seat of the kingdom of Gwynedd, one of the many states into which Wales was divided. Although the Normans occupied the area from 1073 to 1115, in the latter year they were ejected, and the princes of Gwynedd reoccupied the place. But after 1282, Edward I selected Caernarfon to be the center of English rule, and the seat of his son as Prince of Wales. Using some of the material from Segontium, and inspired by the walls of Constantinople that he had seen while on crusade, the king built the magnificent structure we see today. Although seized by Welsh insurgents in 1294, and having fallen to Cromwell's men after a siege in 1646, it has otherwise always remained in the hands of the crown. Thus it has become, depending on your Welsh politics, either a continuing focus of loyalty or an ongoing sign of subjugation.

But it is more. For Caernarfon Castle is, as one might suspect from its history, haunted. There is a phantom lady who has been seen floating through the air and gliding down corridors. Electrical equipment left out overnight at the castle is often found to have been tampered with by agents unknown. Workmen inevitably attribute these occurrences to the "Floating Lady," as they call her.

Caernarfon Castle
Castle Ditch, Caernarfon, Gwynedd LL55 2AY
Wales

Tel: +44 (0) 1286 677617
http://www.caernarfon.com/

Three Spirits Walk

Caerphilly Castle, as it extends over thirty acres, is the largest castle in Wales, dwarfing even Caernarfon. It owes its origin to an Anglo-Norman Marcher Lord, "Red Gilbert" de Clare, Lord of Glamorgan, who built the place in 1268 to secure its surrounding land. De Clare was at the time fighting for the property with Llywelyn ap Gruffudd, Prince of Wales, who would later fall fighting the armies of Edward I. It is an incredibly impressive site, with concentric rings of battlements. These were needed, as the place was attacked even before it was finished, and then subjected to sporadic assaults by various native Welsh nobles.

De Clare was a great enough nobleman in his own right to merit a wedding with Alice de la Marche, the niece of King Henry II. Because her hard-fighting husband was rarely at home (and because of the rather grim and dull nature of the castle itself), Alice organized a jolly round of jousting, feasting, and celebration. At first, the innocent amusements added color to the castle's life, renown to its mistress, and encouragement to happy relations with the locals. The neighboring Welsh nobility were invited to these fetes, and thus able to mingle with the Normans socially. Unhappily, at one of these gatherings, Alice met Tew Teg, a Welsh prince.

Tew Teg was apparently handsomer and younger than Gilbert. Worse still, he was readily at hand, since de Clare was so often away fighting. Lady Alice began an affair with her wild Welshman, and for a period was able to carry it off. But this idyll did not last long. Alice confessed her adultery to a monk, who broke the seal of the confessional and informed her husband. She was packed off to France to live in disgrace with her relations. Outraged, Tew Teg seized the monk and hung him from a tree. In reprisal, de Clare had his wife's former lover killed—although it is interesting to note that he had him assassinated for killing the cleric rather than for his adultery.

In time, the de Clares made way for the Beauchamps, who, in turn, after lavishing a great deal of money on the castle interiors, leased Caerphilly to the Lewises, who took stone from the place to beautify the mansion they were building. Although no one knows for sure how the castle fared during the English Civil War, in the late eighteenth century the place fell into the hands of the marquess of Bute. His descendants, the third and fourth marquesses, being inveterate restorationists, lavished huge sums on Caerphilly. The castle is now in the hands of the government.

This history has left behind certain supernatural remnants. Apparently, after her death in France, Alice de Marche returned to the home she had so disliked in life. Dressed in flowing green robes—in Celtic mythology, green is the color of magic, much beloved by fairies and the like—she can be found gazing to the north from the battlements. She will also float from tower to tower. Once, some schoolboys from the town attempted to catch her. Security guards refuse to go to the flag tower because of the overwhelming smell of perfume that constantly emanates from that haunted spot—a scent they believe belongs to Lady Alice.

But the Green Lady is not the only ghostly excitement offered by Caerphilly Castle. While phantom men-at-arms are sometimes seen on the battlements, a mysterious spirit in red, to whom local legend assigns no identity, is also seen (perhaps as a festive counterpoint to the Green Lady). Most upsetting, however, if encountered, is the *Gwrach-y-rhibyn* of the de Clares.

Among the Welsh, the Gwrach-y-rhibyn is a being in the form of an old woman, like the Irish banshee. Similar to her Irish cousin, the Gwrach-y-rhibyn is attached to specific families, warning them (usually through her bloodcurdling screams) of impending death in the clan. When the de Clares died out, their heraldess of death remained at the castle. Now she is occasionally seen by passersby outside the castle gate; she drifts in, and then vanishes.

Caerphilly has witnessed many strange sights. It is impossible to say whether you'll encounter them. But do try to enter the flag tower—you may get a whiff of the unearthly.

Caerphilly Castle
Caerphilly CF83 1JD
Wales

Tel: +44 (0) 2920 883143
http://www.castlewales.com/caerphil.html
E-mail: www.cadw.wales.gov.uk

The Welsh Capital's Castle

Cardiff Castle has, in some ways, a similar history to Caerphilly. The Romans, followed by the Norman Marcher Lords in 1091, also first occupied Cardiff's site. His younger brother, King Henry I of England, reigned from 1106 until 1134, and imprisoned Robert, Duke of Normandy, here. Robert Le Consol began the transformation of the keep into the castle we see today. The native Welsh under Owen Glendower took the place in 1404. In 1488, it came into the possession of Jasper Tudor—kinsman to Henry, who had become Henry VII after the defeat and death of Richard III at Bosworth Field. As at Caerphilly, powerful ramparts protected rich interiors.

John Crichton-Stuart, the first marquess of Bute, came from an old Scottish noble family. Descendant of kings and hereditary keeper of Rothesay Castle, he acquired Cardiff Castle in the eighteenth century, immediately going to work on its restoration. He died in 1814, leaving as his heir his grandson, John Crichton-Stuart, the second marquess of Bute. Through his encouragement of Cardiff's industry and shipping, as well as his philanthropy, the new master earned both a fortune and the title "Founder of Modern Cardiff." He too undertook further work on the castle, but died rather suddenly at Cardiff in March of 1848, leaving a six-month-old infant as his son and heir.

Nevertheless, this infant, John Patrick Crichton-Stuart, third marquess of Bute, was destined to leave his mark on his country— or rather, on all three countries: England, Wales, and Scotland. Born at Mount Stuart, the family seat on the Scottish island of Bute, the new marquess, armed with an impeccable pedigree, endless wealth, and enormous good taste, underwent the typical schooling for one of his class at Harrow and Oxford. An incredibly erudite man (he mastered languages as far removed from one another as Latin, Greek, Gaelic, and Coptic), the young nobleman also absorbed the mania for all things medieval that enveloped the British upper classes at that time. Having, by the mid-1860s, properly "Gothicized" Mount Stuart, he turned his attention to Caerphilly and Cardiff Castles. In 1868 he shocked his country and his class by converting to Catholicism. From that time on he subsidized the building of churches and monasteries throughout the British Isles. At Cardiff, he hired architect William Burges to turn Cardiff Castle into the Gothic fantasy so admired today.

After he died in 1900, his son, the fourth marquess, continued restoration work on the walls. The castle survived the bombing of Cardiff by the Germans during World War II, and remained intact. At last, in 1947, the marquess gave the castle to the City of Cardiff, who runs it today.

At least one of the Butes did not leave, however. It is perhaps fitting that the second marquess, the man who transformed Cardiff into a major city (and so, under Edward VII, into the capital of Wales) remains behind. His son transformed the dressing room where his father died into a Catholic chapel. From time to time, the second marquess appears at the fireplace of the library (in his time, a doorway), passes through a six-foot-thick wall into a corridor, and through another wall into the chapel. Perhaps to commemorate the time of his passing, at 3:45 A.M., the doors of the main dining room open and shut by themselves. Accompanying this strange action, the lights in that room flash on and off.

The second marquess appeared most notably in early 1976. At that time, a young couple told the castle's then-custodian, Derek Edwards, that "A tall man in a cloak pushed past them in a great hurry. . . [The woman] had been standing at the top of the stairway. . . [and] on turning to her right witnessed a tall figure in a red cloak. The man seemed to be scowling at her and then vanished." Naturally, this figure matched the painting of the second marquess of Bute hanging on a nearby wall.

In addition to His Lordship, in a stockroom near the chapel— where the room's contents are often found mysteriously disorganized—a "faceless vision in a flowing grayish-white skirt" is sometimes seen. Just who or what that may be is unknown.

But strange things happened in the time of the third marquess as well. In November 1868, Mr. John Boyle, a trustee of Lord Bute's father, "seated in the library, heard a carriage roll through the great courtyard and stop at the door. After an interval, thinking the bell must be broken, he came into the hall, but the butler, who was waiting there, assured him that no carriage had come. He only heard later, for the first time, that the arrival of a spectral carriage was said always to foretell the death of some member of the Hastings family, friends and relatives of the Crichton-Stuarts." Mr. Boyle's grandson adds: "My grandfather always told this story very solemnly and with the fullest conviction of its truth, though he was not at all apt to believe in anything except the most positive and material facts."

At the same time, Lady Margaret MacRae, the third marquess's only daughter, declared that on the eve of her father's death at

Dumfries House (a family seat in Ayrshire, Scotland) on October 8, 1900, she heard exactly the same thing.

Derek Edwards experienced his first encounter with a castle ghost in 1975 after working there for a year. After a civic luncheon in the dining room, Edwards was cleaning things up when he saw, at the other end of the hall, a man in the doorway. Walking toward him, Edwards asked, "Can I help you, sir?" The man turned to face him and suddenly vanished. His children and a friend of theirs who was staying with them saw a man looking at them in the bedroom. Doors locked themselves, a wardrobe moved, and the family dog acted crazy.

Considering all that Cardiff Castle was able to provide in terms of hauntings for expatriate Scots like the Crichton-Stuarts, it might very well do even more for visiting Americans. One thing is certain: At Cardiff Castle, history comes alive—literally!

Cardiff Castle
Castle Street
Cardiff CF10 3RB
Wales

Tel: +44 (0) 2920 878100
Fax: +44 (0) 2920 231417
http://www.cardiffcastle.com/castle.htm
E-mail: cardiffcastle@cardiff.gov.uk

Can Another Ghost Be Found?

Best known for its eighteenth-century garden, Powis Castle's origins lie in the early thirteenth century, when the Welsh princes of Powis turned it into a stronghold. The Welsh dubbed it *Y Castell Coch*—the Red Castle—because of the red sandstone employed in much of the early stonework. After various misadventures, Sir Edward Herbert bought Powis Castle in 1587. When Sir Edward bought Powis, he began a restoration that would last until 1595.

Although the Herberts remained loyal to their king during the English Civil War, Sir Thomas Myddelton and his parliamentarian forces captured Powis Castle in 1644. They held on to Powis during the Commonwealth, forcing the Herberts, when they regained their ownership at the Restoration in 1660, to rebuild the place in a finer style than ever before. They transformed Powis from a rough border fortress into a repository of fine furniture and paintings. Although the Herberts supported James II in 1688, the oldest son was able to hold onto the castle when his father went into exile with that king.

Six decades later, the main branch having become extinct, Powis Castle passed to a Protestant cousin, Henry Arthur Herbert. George II in turn named him Earl of Powis. Unfortunately, his business acumen was nil, and the Herbert fortune was depleted fairly rapidly. Luckily, his heiress, Lady Henrietta Herbert, married Edward Clive in 1784. The new son-in-law was the son of Lord Clive of India, and wealthy in his own right—the castle would remain in the family. The treasures Edward brought to Powis constitute the Clive Museum, while the coach house, with its nine-teenth-century state coach and livery, and the aforementioned gardens continue to draw visitors today. Although Powis Castle is now in the hands of the National Trust, the current earl of Powis still lives there.

Powis Castle was the scene of one of the most-often told ghost stories in the principality. Back in 1780, there had been, for some time, a haunted bedroom in the castle. On no account would the veteran servants stay there overnight, but as a cruel joke by the other staff, a new maid was quartered there. The ghost of a very well-dressed gentleman quietly entered the room, looked at her, and as he left, awakened her. Frightened, but nevertheless resolved to see the adventure through, she stood her ground as he repeated the performance a second time. Finally, upon his third entrance, she asked him who he was.

Rather than explain, he asked her to follow him. She did, and they came to a place in the castle where a box was hidden, next to which was its key. The ghost informed her that if she took the two items to the earl, who was then in London, he would not return. After agreeing to this task she watched her visitant vanish. The maid was as good as her word. She brought the box and key to London, and presented them to her master. Although we do not know what the box contained, the fact that she was kept on at

Powis—labor-free—until her death plainly shows that the earl was indeed delighted with its contents. The ghost, needless to say, was never seen again.

But as we have seen, there are few castles that boast only one specter. Who knows? At Powis, you may find another one. It is worth a look.

———————

Powis Castle
Welshpool SY21 8RF
Wales

Tel: +44 (0) 1938 551929
Fax: +44 (0) 1938 554336
http://www.castlewales.com/powis.html

A Manor House
Whose History Still Lives

So far we have dealt with huge castles and great clans in Wales, but the manor houses of the gentry have their own ghostly company to offer. There once was a Roman dwelling on the site of Llancaiach Fawr, but the actual house we see today was built for the Prichard family in 1530. Although the country had calmed down considerably since that time, the new manor house was built with thick walls, so that robbers and other marauders might be driven off. The Prichards continued to grow in wealth and local status through the next three generations, and the house was improved accordingly.

However, the outbreak of the English Civil War in 1642 forced uncomfortable decisions—as with all such conflicts—upon the owner of the manor at the time, Colonel Edward Prichard. At first, in common with most of the Welsh, Prichard remained loyal to the king. In fact, so well known was his loyalty that Charles I himself stayed at Llancaiach Fawr. But the royal cause was faltering, and Prichard turned his coat in the summer of 1645. His new friends

entrusted him with the command of Cardiff Castle, which he managed to hold against his former friends through the siege of 1646.
He fought in several other battles, and was duly rewarded by Oliver
Cromwell when the war ended. His wife bore him no male heir,
however, and after Prichard's death in 1655, the house was let out
to tenants for three centuries, and passed into the ownership of
the Williams family in 1953. They in turn sold it to the Rhymney
Valley District Council in 1979. Afterwards, the Council fully restored the house and turned it into the splendid "living history"
exhibit it is today.

As with Colonial Williamsburg or Plimoth Plantation, costumed actors take on the identities of the past—in this case, 1645,
when Colonel Prichard was contemplating his abandonment of the
king. Visitors are greeted and guided around by his servants, who
chat and answer questions about their local gossip, folkways, and
work. Over all hangs the shadow of the war. In the early part of the
year, the staff are all for the king, but after the master changes
sides in the summer, so do the simple folk portrayed by the actors.
In seventeenth-century Wales, as at other times in history, those
in charge dictated the views of their inferiors.

While today's Llancaiach Fawr Manor hosts costumed actors
doing living history, other figures are also seen. They may be in
period costume, and historical, but they are certainly not "living."
To the left of the manor's entrance is a grand spiral staircase, green
in color. On it, two ghostly children are sometimes seen, although
more often it is their disembodied giggles and laughter that are
heard, as if they are playing some sort of invisible game. Moreover,
these ghostlets—or some other spirits—play pranks on both staff
and tourists. The actresses who play maids are no longer frightened
when their apron strings are pulled open from behind. One of the
actors who plays Prichard's steward was walking down the staircase
one day and put his hand on the rail, only to pull it back when he felt
what he described as the small, cold hand of a child underneath!

One ghost who has been identified is the old housekeeper, Mattie. No one knows exactly how she died, but it cannot have been too pleasant. Those who enter her bedroom—considered *the* most haunted room in the house—feel an incredible weight of sadness when they enter. Even the most macho of male visitors are often seen fleeing the room in tears. Apparently Mattie is happier in the kitchen, where she occasionally appears in a white blouse, baking bread. More often, simply the delicious odor of baking bread will fill the room—always, of course, when the oven is cold and empty.

Frequently, as visitors and staff make their way through the house, they will hear voices chatting away in the room ahead of them. But when the living enter said room, the conversation has already moved on into the next chamber, or even upstairs. Either way, the chatter will continue for some time. At one point, a camera crew filmed a lengthy television segment at Llancaiach Fawr, and they were understandably excited by the prospect of further work arising from the connection with such a major production. But when the piece finally aired, it was much shorter than anyone remembered. What had happened? The television company replied that much of the soundtrack had been unusable, as it had been ruined by loud voices, speaking in a foreign language, which drowned out the talk of the interviewers and guests. None who had taken part had heard such voices during the filming, but some speculate that the foreign language was the Welsh spoken in the region during the seventeenth century.

Although Llancaiach Fawr has more than its share of disembodied voices—one visitor was told "Out, out!" by a patch of air—they are rarely abusive, as is often the case at other places. This is good, because every room in the house seems to have its phantoms. Even the stairs on the porch have their residents: children once more, and typically heard far more often than seen. One of them who does put in the odd visual appearance is a small black boy. African children were often kept like pets in the homes of the wealthy in the seventeenth century. This one appears to have been happy, although the climate may well have killed him, as it did so many of his brethren.

It would be manifestly unfair if the servants alone were forced to come back and haunt Llancaiach Fawr. But justice seems to prevail. Apparently the man in Jacobean clothes who now and then is seen sitting in a window ledge in the great hall is none other than Colonel Prichard himself. As with the other specters in this haunted house, for every sighting there are scores of sound effects. Much more frequent than sightings are the sounds of heavy footsteps, said to be those of Colonel Pritchard, meditating on switching allegiances, pacing back and forth through the hall. So heavy are these steps that during refurbishment in the 1980s, the new plaster in the kitchen ceiling just below the hall kept falling down. There was no logical reason for it. The affected area was restricted to the portion directly beneath the spot where the footsteps are heard.

In the granary, a child who died there opens wardrobe doors and pulls visitors' long hair. The small room next to Maggie's offers a woman who stands in the window, to the surprise of visitors in the garden below. Even the road outside is haunted, as drivers who have been frightened by the tall man in black hat and cloak can attest.

"Living History" presentations are becoming ever more popular, in Europe and America. But, if you really want to interact with the past—both the living and the dead—Llancaiach Fawr is definitely the place to do it!

Llancaiach Fawr Manor
Nelson, Treharris CF46 6ER
Wales

Tel: +44 (0) 1443 412248
http://www.caerphilly.gov.uk/visiting/museums/
*   llancaiachfawrmanor.htm*

Flames in the Parlor

Another fine old haunted manor house in Wales is Aberglasney. Although we do not know when it was built, the bard Lewis Glyn Cothi wrote an ode about it as early as 1471. In 1600, the house was sold to Anthony Rudd, the Anglican bishop of St. David's. Although the married bishop intended that his family should occupy the house permanently, within a century growing debt forced them to sell. This became a recurring theme for the house, as dynasty after dynasty bought the place, went broke in a few decades, and had to sell. Nevertheless, each family left improvements.

In the eighteenth century, the Dyer clan occupied the place, beginning a spurt of building that saw the medieval house redone in the Queen Anne style. The Dyers were forced to sell in 1798.

In 1801, upon his retirement from the East India Company, Thomas Phillips bought Aberglasney, and added a large Ionic portico to the entrance front. Having spent three decades as a "nabob" in India, Phillips was used to a lavish lifestyle. Despite his extravagance, however, Phillips escaped the financial curse of

Aberglasney, leaving the house and a tidy fortune to his heirs (none of whom were his children). Unfortunately, this good fortune was not to last. For Phillips's successors, misfortune followed misfortune, as successive owners faced barren marriages, the death of beloved children, and financial ruin.

Still, the house itself did well enough. By the turn of the century, Aberglasney had passed to Phillips's collateral descendant, Mrs. Marianne Mayhew. Her horticulturally minded husband collected and then successfully planted a large number of rare specimen trees. Many of these survive today, giving the gardens their unique atmosphere. Still here also is the thousand-year-old yew tunnel, the oldest living garden wonder in Europe.

But a series of misfortunes at last led to the house's abandonment in the 1960s. Weeds and nettles invaded the grounds, while the house was besieged by damp, dry rot, and vandalism. By the 1990s Aberglasney was derelict. In 1995, however, the Aberglasney Restoration Trust bought the property and began the ongoing restoration which has returned the estate to its former glory.

The work of restoration did more than awaken the house; it seems that other things were awoken as well. Restorers working on the house often saw a young girl in a corner of the basement, cooking nonexistent food. Guides walking through the cloisters would hear footsteps behind them, turn around, and see nothing. The house had risen from the dead, and apparently, so had its permanent inhabitants.

As far back as the time of the Rudds, uncanny stories have gathered around Aberglasney. The earliest told were of the floating candle flames that appear before any deaths in the house—always the same number as those about to die. In the 1630s, a housekeeper saw five such lights floating in the Blue Room. Shortly thereafter, five maids who were sleeping there died, either by suffocation from coal fumes or else from arsenic poisoning due to the room's fresh paint. To this day, people unaware of this story report becoming frightened for no reason in the Blue Room. Back in the 1930s, a gardener's assistant, while cutting ivy from the window area on the exterior of the Blue Room, quickly sped down his ladder. He reported that "Victorian-dressed ladies" had been peering out at him. There were, of course, no such women in the house.

However much grief Aberglasney has brought most of its owners, apparently Thomas Phillips is as happy there in death as he was in life. Shortly after his demise in 1824, he began his posthumous wanderings through the house and grounds, and has appeared to gardeners, staff, visitors, and tradesmen ever since. He never seems unhappy or upset, and brings no sense of fear or sadness to his viewers.

The same cannot be said about the thing that lurks in Pigeon House Wood, to the rear of the estate. At a certain spot approaching the wood, a number of visitors begin to feel very uneasy. As they descend the dirt path to the edge of the wood, they become fearful, at which point a feeling of coldness descends upon them. Nothing uncanny has ever been seen there, but it is remarkable that so many people have experienced these precise feelings at this very same spot.

Aberglasney has been described as simultaneously serene, tragic, and beautiful. Certainly it is all three by turns. In a sense, the house, gardens, and their history are a microcosm of the human experience as a whole—thus, it comes as no surprise that its ghosts reflect the same diversity. Certainly, it is worth a visit by those seeking a full range of haunting.

Aberglasney
Llangathen, Carmarthenshire SA32 8QH
Wales

Tel: +44 (0) 1558 668998
http://www.aberglasney.org.uk
E-mail:info@aberglasney.org.uk

In the Goblin Tower

Denbigh Castle owes its present incarnation to that great fortress builder, Edward I. As with his keeps at Caernarfon, Conwy, Harlech, and Beaumaris, this castle was built to keep down the native Welsh in a strategic location the locals themselves had previously occupied.

As early as the commencement of the thirteenth century, the princes of Gwynedd maintained a stronghold on the present site of the castle. But in 1282, Edward seized Denbigh from its defenders, and began construction of the impressive fortress we see today. He immediately granted the lordship of Denbigh to one of his most trusted and valiant captains, Henry de Lacy, the Earl of Lincoln. Although in ruins now, it remains an extraordinary example of medieval castle building. By 1284, Denbigh Castle dominated its surroundings. De Lacy did not see the Castle completed before his death in 1311, but this did not matter; Denbigh had accomplished its goal of subduing the area.

The Castle continued to carry out the maintenance of the king's peace until 1646, when the Civil War swept over the area. The royalist garrison prepared to hold out, which they managed to do for four months. Much of the devastation we see now dates from that time—either from the violence of the siege itself, or the partial dismantling done by the parliamentary army to prevent the royalist Welsh from reoccupying it.

One of the towers built by de Lacy was the Goblin Tower, erected to protect the castle's water supply. It so happened that one day his fifteen-year-old son was curious to see how the construction was progressing. As he walked about the scaffolding, he slipped and fell to his doom, dying instantly. Many people since have seen his unhappy face staring from a window in the Goblin Tower.

Perhaps this is because he has a good view of the doings of another phantom that haunts the surrounding footpaths—the mysterious "White Lady." Dressed in a shawl and surrounded by a glowing white haze, she has frightened many. In December 1999, three terrified lads saw her standing at the foot of Goblin Tower. She then slowly glided down the hill toward them. Little as we know of her, we know even less of a medieval soldier who recently appeared in a photo standing behind two friends. Of course, no such person was actually standing there at the time!

The purely residential sections of the castle have been roofless and ruinous for a long time. Even so, Denbigh Castle still offers shelter to its long-term residents.

Denbigh Castle
Castle Hill, Denbigh, Clwyd CF1 3NQ
Wales

Tel: +44 (0) 1745 813385
http://www.denbigh.com/castle.html

The Stench Lingers On

The triumph of the English did not mean the end of the Welsh princes; far from it. Instead, their descendants adapted to the new order of things, many becoming mere gentry. Bereft of national power, they remained players on the local scene. Typical of these was the Wynn clan, who descend from the princes of Gwynedd. Howell Coetmore, who fought under the Black Prince as commander of longbowmen at the Battle of Poitiers in 1356, built Gwydir Castle, their ancient seat. After the Wars of the Roses, Meredith, founder of the Wynn dynasty and a leading supporter of King Henry VII, rebuilt the castle in 1490. Gwydir was transformed from fortified house to elegant Tudor residence in the 1540s by Morris Wynn.

The Wynns, although they had lost their princely status, long remained one of the more important Welsh families. Retaining their Catholicism longer than most, the Wynns were implicated in such affairs as the Babington Plot in 1586 and the Gunpowder

Plot in 1605. If no longer royalty themselves, the Wynns entertained kings, queens, and princes. Among others, Gwydir has seen King Charles I in September 1645; King George V and Queen Mary, when they were still duke and duchess of York in 1899; and HRH, the Prince of Wales in 1998. Prince Charles was on hand to open the newly reinstalled 1640s dining room, which had been sold to William Randolph Hearst, donated to the Metropolitan Museum in New York, and eventually restored to its original home in 1996.

By the late twentieth century the house had become almost a ruin, covered in vines, frequently the scene of late-night raves. But a young couple, Judy Corbett and Peter Welford, discovered the place, put every penny they had into it, and brought it back from the dead. They traced the location of the dining-room panels, and the museum allowed their return to Wales. It was the opening of the restored room that brought Prince Charles to Gwydir. But as might be expected, making Gwydir live again meant exposing the living to the castle's ghosts—some of whom had appeared as early as the nineteenth century.

In the north wing is a room called the "Ghost Room." In the nineteenth century, this room was the scene of appearances by a white or gray lady, who would haunt both the room and the nearby corridor. She was inevitably accompanied by the smell of rotting flesh. She has not been seen in some years, but visitors reported feeling her touch on their shoulders, and the horrible stench continues to emanate at times from the areas she walked. It is said that either the first or fifth baronet (both called Sir John) had an affair with a castle serving maid when he was young. The relationship became inconvenient for the young man, so he murdered the girl, depositing her corpse in a walled-up space in one of the chimney breasts. The stench lingered on for a long time. During the course of the twentieth century, a hollowed-out space was found within the large chimney breast backing onto the Ghost

Room at the hall end of the passage. This spot is where the smell is always at its strongest.

Although the first Sir John was thought of as a mild-mannered antiquarian outside the area, locals maintain to this day that the spirit of the old baronet lies trapped beneath the waterfall near Betws-y-Coed called the Swallow Falls. There, he is "forever to be purged, purified, and spat upon (by the waters) for the evil deeds committed by him in his days of nature." Whether or not he is living under the waterfall, he has been seen on the spiral staircase that leads from the Solar Hall to the Great Chamber.

There are a large number of other ghosts that have been reported, such as invisible children crying, a ghost dog (to whom are ascribed bones found in the cellar in 1995), and a phantom procession on nocturnal parade on the Great Terrace, near Sir John's arch. There is also an unknown gentleman in an "Edwardian-style suit" who has been seen by visitors several times, most notably in 1975 and in 1978. Could he be the marquess of Lincolnshire, returned to see his property protected? Who knows—what is certain is that the resurrection of Gwydir Castle is in itself as remarkable as any ghost story.

Gwydir Castle
Llanrwst LL26 0PN
North Wales

Tel/Fax: + 44 (0) 1492 641687
http://www.gwydir-castle.co.uk/
E-mail: info@gwydircastle.co.uk

Scotland Forever . . . and Ever?

S *cotland forever!* Even today, these words rouse the hearts of millions of Scots and their descendants across the globe. In the United States, Canada, Australia, New Zealand, South Africa, and the West Indies, the sons of Alba thrill to the bagpipes, the tartan, the kilt, and, of course, Scotch whiskey (it should be noted that "Scotch" *only* refers to the drink; the people themselves are Scots). Throughout the English-speaking world, Highland games are played, Burns and Saint Andrew's Night dinners consumed, and clan relationships prized. Moreover, Scottish regiments in the armies of four of the above-named "old Dominions"— the Black Watch of Canada, the New South Wales Scottish, the New Zealand Scottish, and the Cape Town Highlanders—keep the military traditions of their fathers' homeland alive.

Why the fascination with such a small country? Much of it has to do with the romantic (or at least exciting) course of Scots history. Above all, it is a tale of lost causes and ultimate survival that continues to tug at the heart, despite defeat. The first people we know of in Scotland, the Picts, successfully resisted the Roman legions, the only such folk to do so in all the island of Britain. When the Irish invaders of Scotland's northwest (ironically called "Scots" themselves) settled down on their land, they introduced the Gaelic language that, until the eighteenth century, dominated the highlands and islands of the country. The Britons, like their brothers in Wales, Cornwall, and adjoining Cumbria, were forced into the region called Strathclyde by the Anglo-Saxon Northumbrians, who carved out Lothian as their home. These four peoples warred against each other until they were united in the ninth century by Kenneth MacAlpin, the first "King of Scots."

But this union was always a bit tenuous. On the border with England, turbulent lords flourished as they did on the southern side. In the lowlands there were lairds, each jealous of his neighbor, and in the Highlands, wild clan chiefs, many of them a match for the king himself in terms of soldiers and lands. Every one of these individuals needed a castle. So it is that literally hundreds of them dot the Scottish countryside.

Overshadowing the innumerable petty feuds of the Scottish chiefs was the country's struggle to maintain its independence from England. Disunity, the Celtic curse, severely hampered the attempts of successive Scots kings to resist English occupation. But the various royal houses produced individuals whose names still conjure images of brave deeds and desperate loyalty: Robert the Bruce, Mary Queen of Scots, and Bonnie Prince Charlie, for example.

Against this warlike backdrop was the omnipresent Celtic imagination. As in Wales, Ireland, and the other Celtic lands, fairies, witches, seers, and the like peopled the sparsely settled landscape. Omens both good and bad abounded, as did holy wells and sacred mountains.

Given both the history and mental setting of Scotland, we would not be too surprised if most Scots castles offered up a ghost or two—and so they do. Choosing has been a bit hard. But as you will see, hauntings are as Scottish as haggis!

Setting for Tragedy

If ever a place was the focus of Scots national history over the past five decades, Her Majesty's Palace of Holyrood is it. As with the country itself, the story of the place is one of tragedy broken up by occasional, all-too-brief bouts of merriment. Holyrood owes its origin to a vision King David I had back in 1128. One day, while out hunting, he had a vision of a stag. It attacked him, but the king was very much surprised to see a crucifix he recognized as belonging to his mother (who was later canonized as Saint Margaret of Scotland) between its antlers. Inspired by this apparition, he founded an Augustinian monastery on the site, which he named Holyrood (Holy Cross) Abbey. The abbey's symbol would be a stag's head with a cross between its antlers, in commemoration of the strange apparition the king had witnessed.

In time, due to its location, the town of Edinburgh became the capital of Scotland. But the Royal Castle of Edinburgh set high up on the rock, although a great defensive structure, was none too comfortable. So, in 1501 James IV built a palace adjoining the abbey for himself and his bride, Margaret Tudor (the sister of Henry VIII). His son, James V, made extensive renovations between 1528 and 1536. The result was a luxurious residence, fit for his new wife, Madelaine, daughter of King François I of France. Unhappily, the cold climate of her new home did not agree with her, and her life as queen was short. In need of an heir, James married Mary of Guise, and had her crowned queen in Holyrood Abbey. James himself died just after the birth of his only child—a daughter.

This daughter grew up to be Mary Queen of Scots (1542–1587), a tragic figure if ever there was one. Promptly affianced to the young dauphin of France, she was packed off to her future husband's country as soon as possible—as much for her safety from the turbulent Scots lords as anything else. She was educated at the French court, while her mother acted as regent in Scotland.

While the canny Mary of Guise was able to hold together a semblance of order, things were stirring under the surface, most notably the Protestant revolt. Many of the Scots lords, noting how much in the way of church property had come into the hands of the English nobility after Henry VIII broke with Rome, began licking their chops. The new doctrines were being spread by the eloquent (if unpleasant) preacher, John Knox. In the midst of this intrigue, Mary's husband, François II, ascended the French throne, and Mary was made queen of both Scotland and France. Two years later, however, both her mother and husband died. She returned to Scotland.

The greatest dramas of her seven-year reign were played out at Holyrood: her confrontations with the misogynistic Knox and his noble allies; her marriage to the effete Lord Darnley; the murder of her secretary, David Rizzio, before her eyes; and her forced marriage to Lord Bothwell. Finally, in 1567, after the defeat of her and Bothwell's army at Langside, she was forced to flee to England.

There, her cousin Elizabeth kept her in a series of prisons, until at last ordering her judicial murder in 1587.

Holyrood was neglected during the minority of Mary's son, James VI. This was even more the case after he succeeded Elizabeth I on the English throne (as James I) in 1603. The place was renovated when he returned in 1617, and more improvements were carried out in 1633, when James's son, Charles I, was crowned King of Scots at St. Giles in Edinburgh. During the Civil War, Holyrood was occupied by Cromwell's troops, but the restoration that Charles II carried out involved extensive repairs. After his brother, James, Duke of York, became a Catholic, he took up residence at Holyrood, transforming the abbey into the Chapel Royal and restoring it to Catholic worship.

He in turn came to the throne as James VII of Scotland and II of England in 1685. Three years later he was deposed and replaced with his son-in-law and daughter, William and Mary. Even though exiled, he and his descendants still worked with their supporters—the Jacobites—for their restoration. Although the Edinburgh mob had sacked the abbey at news of James's overthrow, many of the citizens of the town remained loyal.

The new regime divided Holyrood into "grace and favor" apartments such as those at Hampton Court. In 1745, Bonnie Prince Charlie, grandson of James VII and son of James VIII, landed in Scotland, roused the country, occupied Edinburgh, and proclaimed his father king. Holyrood was again the center of a glittering court, and it seemed that the old grandeur had been restored. But it all ended rather quickly, with the Jacobites' defeat at the hands of George II's army at Culloden the following year.

Holyrood slipped back into a slumber, from which it awoke briefly in 1822, during the reign of George IV, when that king traveled north dressed in the Highland garb forbidden since Culloden. He gave orders that Mary Queen of Scots's apartments were to be preserved exactly as they had been.

Queen Victoria, who had bought a private residence at Balmoral, began once again staying at Holyroodhouse, throwing garden parties, conducting investitures and banquets and the like. This her successors have kept up, so that, for at least a small part of the year, Holyroodhouse is once again the center of a royal court. But in some ways, its earlier history remains, full-time.

Of this history, those events surrounding the tragic life of Mary Queen of Scots are perhaps the most poignant. The murder of David Rizzio was a tremendous shock to the young Mary. An Italian, he seems to have shared (along with Mary's husband, Lord Darnley) a preference for his own gender. Nevertheless, Darnley became increasingly jealous of his wife's relationship with Rizzio— which, after all, had begun when she was in France. Moreover, those Scots nobility who were keen on running (and plundering) the country themselves objected to Rizzio's support of his employer. Whatever the lack of romance between the two, there is no doubt that he was the strongest shoulder available to her. The nobles played on Darnley's jealousy, and convinced him that Rizzio should be murdered.

Darnley and a group of his confederates broke into the queen's apartments one night in 1566. Before Mary's horrified eyes, they seized Rizzio and stabbed him over and over. The floor was covered with bloodstains, which to this day cannot be removed. If Darnley thought the removal of his wife's secretary in this fashion would somehow endear him to her, he was much mistaken. The ambiance in this room remains oppressive, and one current member of the royal family declared that the chamber has a "terrible atmosphere."

Nor did the Protestant lords get what they wanted; all they discovered was that Mary had not needed Rizzio to continue to act decisively. Worse still, they could not control her through Darnley, and Darnley himself, with Rizzo out of the way, began to act independently of them. There was even some fear of reconciliation between him and his wife. He was inconvenient to them, to say the least. What was convenient, however, was the way his house at Kirk o' Field blew up barely a year after Rizzio's murder. Such an unpleasant death must surely leave some trace behind, and sure enough, this one did. The apartment where Darnley received guests at Holyroodhouse is often host to strange shadows, much to the annoyance of visitors and staff.

The Queen's Audience Chamber, where Mary received her guests, sometimes features a "gray lady." She stands near one of the staircases, looking rather indistinct; the features of her face are never visible. Said to have been one Mary's friends, she might have been one of the four Marys—Mary Seaton, Mary Beaton, Mary Fleming, or Mary Hamilton—ladies-in-waiting to the queen who shared many of her unpleasant adventures. In any case, royal employees often encounter the Gray Lady when the court uses this wing as office space during Queen Elizabeth II's annual sojourn in the Scots capital. Perhaps the Gray Lady is checking to see that the current monarch's retinue serves her mistress's descendant as loyally as Mary's did her.

The other particularly haunted place in the palace is the Long Gallery, with its painting of Scots kings. Invisible footsteps are heard there by staff and visitors; but on at least one occasion, a ghost was seen. A window cleaner doing his job on the exterior of the gallery one autumn day lowered the top half of the window he was washing, only to see the bearded face of a man in a Renaissance-era white ruff collar and black cloak, staring back at him. The cleaner (who owned the company, as it turned out) quickly sped down the ladder and back to his car. He did not regret forfeiting his contract with the palace.

Edinburgh's palace is a fascinating place, to be sure. To walk its floors puts the visitor into an almost tangible relationship with those who paced them before. Holyroodhouse offers compelling testimony that while human glory does not last, the consequences of trying to attain it very well might.

Palace of Holyroodhouse
Canongate
Royal Mile
Edinburgh EH8 8DX
Scotland

Tel: +44 (0) 1315 565100
Fax: +44 (0) 2079 309625
http://www.aboutbritain.com/PalaceofHolyroodhouse.htm
http://www.royal.gov.uk/output/page559.asp
E-mail: holyroodhouse@royalcollection.org.uk

Where Scotland's Crown
is Guarded

I f Holyroodhouse is the Scottish capital's equivalent of Bucking-
ham Palace, then surely Edinburgh Castle is its answer to the
Tower of London. On the opposite end of the Royal Mile from
the palace, this stronghold was nearly impregnable, given its high
location on the Castle Rock. As the Mile wends its way down to
Holyrood, it passes the old Parliament Building and St. Giles'
Cathedral, symbols of the two other institutions that shared power
with the crown in the days of Scots independence.

But where Holyrood was the symbol of the wealth and splendor
of Scottish kings, the castle was their stronghold. Here were kept
things too precious to be exposed to any possible danger. In an extremely informative modern display, the Honors of Scotland—the
Scots crown jewels—are kept here, as they have been for centuries,
save during the time they were hidden from Oliver Cromwell, and
when they were placed elsewhere for safety during World War II.
The year 1997 saw the arrival of the Stone of Scone, the rock slab

upon which Scots kings were crowned until Edward I took it to London and placed it in his coronation chair at Westminster Abbey, back in the seventeenth century. In this powerful refuge, Mary Queen of Scots gave birth to King James VI (later England's James I), as no other place in the country was thought to be safe enough. The continued presence of the military garrison is signaled six days a week by the firing of the gun at 1:00 P.M.

Castle Rock was a stronghold even before the Romans made their unsuccessful attempt to conquer the area. The core of the complex is St. Margaret's Chapel, built over nine hundred years ago by the Scots queen whose sanctity was proverbial among her people. Although the fortifications on the rock have several times been demolished—most notably by Robert the Bruce, to keep the fortress out of English hands—the chapel has been spared each time.

Since then, a new network of fortifications has gradually been erected, resulting in an incredibly impressive stronghold. Only the advent of modern weaponry has diminished the castle's sense of impregnability. Beneath these battlements is a series of vaults, only recently re-excavated, which served, among other things, as holding pens for various prisoners of war.

Edinburgh Castle has withstood many sieges. Oliver Cromwell took the place during the Civil War. In 1688, the authorities declared victory for the invading William of Orange, who deposed James VIII and II in England. The mob celebrated, as we have seen, by plundering the Catholic Chapel Royal at Holyrood Abbey, as well as by ejecting the Anglican congregation from St. Giles' Cathedral (these last founded the church of Old St. Paul's in response, ever after a seat of Jacobite loyalties). But the Duke of Gordon continued to hold the castle for King James, until he and his soldiers were starved out. From Castle Rock the duke greeted the king's other great champion, John Graham of Claverhouse, Viscount Dundee (called "Bonnie Dundee"), as he made his way out of the city to lead the Jacobites to victory and his own death at the Battle of Killiecrankie. Ironically, when Bonnie Prince Charlie occupied the city in 1745 and returned Holyroodhouse to its role as center of the court, he was unable to dislodge the Whig soldiers from the Castle.

With such dramatic events on the castle's résumé, it is no wonder that ghostly events continue there today. Some are of long standing. A few centuries ago, a network of tunnels under the castle leading to the Royal Mile (and to Holyroodhouse, some theorized) was unearthed, and a piper was sent in to explore. He was to keep playing the bagpipes, so as to alert those on the surface of his status as well as the route and length of the tunnel. Off he went, the other soldiers following him above ground, able to hear his faint notes. Sure enough, he proceeded along the Royal Mile; but halfway to the palace, the piping stopped. After a rescue party found that he had simply vanished, they decided to seal the tunnel back up. But from that midway spot, folks still hear his notes from time to time, on quiet days when the traffic is light.

Visitors also occasionally hear the beating of an invisible drum, even though the drummer has not been seen in centuries. This is because he has always been a harbinger of attack upon the castle, and that has not happened since 1650. After Charles I was beheaded in 1649, strange signs were seen around Edinburgh. After the New Year, meteors in the shape of swords hung in the sky, and ghostly troops of horses rode over the nearby hills. The culmination came when a phantom drummer beat the rounds of the battlements every night. Some sentries reported seeing a spectral boy playing the drum. What made him unusual was that he had no head! This was, of course, associated in the popular mind with the murder of King Charles the year before.

So disturbing were the reports that one night, Colonel Walter Dundas, governor of the castle, decided to man the walls himself. Although he saw no apparition, he did hear the drum beating an old Scots war tune. Accompanying this sound was that of many booted feet marching, and the jangle of weaponry. This invisible procession came nigh to the governor, passed by him, and then faded away. While this was happening, Cromwell's men seized the castle.

During the siege of the castle following the revolution of 1688, heralds summoned the Duke of Gordon to surrender. This His Grace consistently refused to do as long as there was any hope of the king being victorious, and so, 1688 passed into 1689. At last, when the duke decided—even though Bonnie Dundee was still at large—that relief would not be forthcoming, he surrendered on June 13 of that year. One of Gordon's officers was the earl of Balcarres. He was immediately imprisoned in the same castle he had helped defend. On the night of July 27, while lying in bed, he saw his bed curtains drawn back. There appeared his old friend, Dundee, "as beautiful as when he lived, with his long, dark, curled locks streaming down over his laced buff coat and his left hand on his right spule-blade, to hide the wound that the silver bullet had made." The apparition said nothing and vanished, the earl vainly calling after him. He learned afterwards that Dundee had died that day on the field of Killiecrankie, thus dooming James's cause in Scotland.

Not all the ghosts of Edinburgh Castle are human. A phantom hound prowls the dog cemetery at the castle, and has more frequently been heard than seen. French prisoners from the Seven Years War and rebel prisoners from the American Revolution have also made their appearance.

During the 1980s, underground vaults were discovered at the castle. In short order, five of these dungeons were considered to be haunted, with over three hundred ghostly experiences recorded since their discovery. In 2001, a skeptical scientist, Dr. Richard Wiseman of the University of Hertfordshire, undertook an in-depth investigation of the vaults, complete with sophisticated equipment.

What he found was rather interesting. Studying the reactions of visitors who had no prior knowledge of their reputation, Wiseman and his assistants found that the five "most haunted" vaults accounted for the majority of odd experiences within their control group. Of the 250 visitors asked to stand in any one of the ten vaults for as many minutes, 44 percent reported something unusual. Dr Wiseman said: "What was interesting for us was whether or not those experiences would stack up in the vaults with the reputation for being haunted, and the answer is that that definitely does happen."

Among the reported happenings were temperature changes; burning, touching, and pulling sensations; and the sound of breathing. There was also a sighting: one woman saw a man in a leather apron walking across the doorway. Ultimately, Dr. Wiseman attributed all of these things to the effect of lighting in the five "haunted vaults."

The castle continues to dole out the strange in good measure to its denizens. In *The Scotsman* newspaper on February 22, 2003, an article by David Lee reported that "Builders carrying out a renovation project at Edinburgh Castle claim their labors are being disturbed—by the ghosts of prisoners from the Napoleonic Wars." The article went on to say that photos of the men working on renovations at the Queen Anne building in the castle had caught rather hazy blue orbs floating over the workers' heads. Many of the builders refused to be left alone, and the contractor consulted a medium. Some of them asked for "a special canopy to shield them from the glare of ghostly eyes gazing down on them." The site manager, Willie Hamilton, told the paper, "I can feel a presence whenever I am alone in the site office. It is as if someone is above me, looking down as I work. It is very spooky."

For centuries, Edinburgh Castle has served to defend Scotland's capital against all manner of enemies. But, as this particular event shows, neither men nor tall ramparts can keep out the supernatural.

Edinburgh Castle
Castlehill
Edinburgh E11 1SG
Scotland

Tel: +44 (0) 1312 259846
Fax: +44 (0) 1312 204733
http://www.edinburghcastle.biz/
E-mail: hs.explorer@scotland.gsi.gov.uk

Ruined Splendor

Linlithgow Palace, one of the favorite residences of the ill-starred Stuart dynasty, is now a ruin. Nevertheless, more than enough remains to show its grandeur. Its apartments cluster around a central courtyard, in the French Renaissance manner—underscoring the relationship between the Stuarts and their French allies. James I began the building of the place, as well as the Church of St. Michael, which remains in use today (albeit for a Presbyterian congregation), and which traditionally served as a Chapel Royal for the family. The huge Great Hall still remains partially intact, and its fireplace was restored in 1906. The west range, when completed, contained new royal apartments for James IV and his queen, Margaret Tudor; as the daughter of English King Henry VII, she would find her loyalties divided.

James V added further details, including the present gatehouse. Although the internal decorations and furnishings are gone, with the help of surviving palaces like Holyroodhouse and Falkland, it is easy to imagine what Linlithgow looked like in its prime. Made for elegance, in reflection of the greatness of the Scots Crown, it was compared by Mary of Guise, consort of James V and mother of Mary Queen of Scots, to the most splendid in France.

Mary of Scots herself was born here in 1542, although within seven months she was sent to Stirling Castle for safety. To escape both Henry VIII's and the Protestant Scots nobility's plans for her, Mary went to France as the betrothed of the dauphin when she was six. But after her return in 1560, Linlithgow became one of her favorite residences; she stayed here many times over the seven years of active rule she would enjoy.

Although her son James visited here once before he became King of England in 1603, the place was sadly neglected. He made one other visit, in 1617, with his son, Charles. Charles I would return in 1633, on the occasion of his coronation in Edinburgh. Cromwell spent the winter of 1650 to 1651 at the palace, during his conquest of Scotland. From then until 1745, Linlithgow was allowed to deteriorate. But in that year Bonnie Prince Charlie arrived. As at Holyroodhouse, his stay meant a revival of the shimmering splendor that had once characterized the Scots court. But the dream fizzled, and when the army of George II, commanded by his son, the Duke of Cumberland (called "Butcher Cumberland" on account of his winning ways), arrived at Linlithgow, they used the palace as a barracks. They left the palace and marched north on February 1, 1746, bound for Culloden where the Jacobite cause would go down. Meanwhile, one of Cumberland's troops had left an unattended fire that soon spread. After the flames subsided, the palace was a roofless shell.

So it has remained. Yet it has also retained its legal status as a royal palace. King George V held court there in 1914, and seriously considered restoring it—World War I absorbed the necessary funding, however. The surrounding property, including a loch and a *pele* (or stockade), remains a royal park and still has its own police force.

In any case, the ghosts of the place are not aware of any changes in status. As mentioned, near the palace is St. Michael's Church. This building was not yet completed in 1513, when James IV contemplated going to war against his brother-in-law, Henry VIII. As he prayed for guidance, a spirit appeared, and warned him not to go to war against England. He would have done well to listen; the flower of the Scots nobility and he himself were cut down at the Battle of Flodden Field. Not only would his country have to suffer under a regency as a result (his son, James V, being a minor), but precisely those nobles who would have upheld his granddaughter, the best leaders in the country, were lost—thus paving the way for the tragedy of Mary's reign.

For Queen Margaret, the battle at Flodden could not have a good outcome, resulting, as it must, in the defeat of either her husband or her brother. She waited in vain for James to return from the battle in the drafty lookout post above the northwest turnpike stair, called today "Queen Margaret's bower." She must have been in agony, although after receiving the dreaded news of her husband's death, the following year she married Archibald Douglas, sixth earl of Angus, and fled Scotland with him. Even so, she has returned, and her ghost is sometimes seen by visitors in the "bower" that bears her name.

There is one other well-known spirit who walks at Linlithgow: the "Blue Lady." A number of people, including a former custodian, have seen her near the main entrance. She is seen striding intently toward the church, but she disappears within a few feet of the wall. She is usually seen at about 9:00 A.M. in April, but also occasionally in September. While no one knows her identity, we can imagine that perhaps she is the very spirit who warned James V!

Unlike Holyroodhouse, Linlithgow is a ruin—but in a spectral sense, it is very much alive. However that may be, it is well worth visiting. Perhaps red roses will soothe the Blue Lady's anger!

Linlithgow Palace
Kirkgate, Linlithgow
West Lothian EH49 7AL
Scotland

Tel: +44 (0) 1506 842896
http://www.aboutscotland.com/linlith/gow.html

Scotland's Strongbox

Stirling Castles lies astride the "waist" of Scotland; control of this fortress was considered the key to controlling the country. While there is no proof that either the Picts or the Romans fortified the rock the castle stands on, it is sure that they fought over it. There are even tales of King Arthur's conquest of the place—some scholars have attempted to identify Stirling with Camelot! What is certain is that warriors have attacked or besieged the castle sixteen times, and fought three battles nearby, while another battle was waged a few miles north. The castle has served as a place for baptism, coronation, and burial for a number of Scots kings. One king, James II, committed murder here, and another king, James III, was murdered nearby.

The greater part of Stirling was built between 1496 and 1583, thanks to James IV, V, and VI, and to Mary of Guise, consort of James V. Among other features, the castle boasts a palace built by James V, and a Chapel Royal. As an infant, Mary Queen of Scots was crowned in the old chapel in 1543, and made a number of visits after her return from France.

The queen herself had an uncanny experience here. At a time when Mary and her retinue were staying at Stirling, one of her maids dreamt that the queen's life was in danger. She woke up and rushed to Mary's bedroom, only to find her bed curtains aflame and the queen fast asleep inside. Once she was safe, Mary remembered a prophecy that she would one day face death by fire while at Stirling.

The castle retains quite a company of ghosts. The best known (and most far ranging) is the Green Lady. Quite capable of appearing almost anywhere and at any time, she delayed dinner in the Officers' Mess (Stirling still retains a garrison) when she appeared behind the chef in the kitchen. Feeling watched, he turned around, only to see her green vapory form staring at his handiwork. Before she could offer any helpful suggestions, he fainted.

Wherever and whenever she appears, however, the Green Lady is often a harbinger of disaster. Several fires and other mishaps have occurred shortly after her appearance. But sometimes, as in the kitchen episode, nothing happens. It may be that on this particular occasion, she prevented the officers of the Argyll and Sutherland Highlanders from suffering severe indigestion.

Battlements formerly surmounted the Governor's Block, as the upper square of the castle is called. In the 1820s sentries walking their beat began reporting strange sights and sounds. At last, a sentry taking over guard duty one night found the guardsman he was supposed to replace lying dead at his post, his mouth wide open and a look of absolute terror on his face. In the ensuing decades, sentry duty there was halted and the battlements dismantled, leaving only a peaked roof upon which no one can walk. Nevertheless, in the room directly below, footsteps are sometimes heard walking across the ceiling, as though a sentry was still making his rounds. This was first reported in 1946 and again a decade later by two different officers of the Argyll and Sutherlands, on two separate nights. In all three cases, the realization that there was nowhere for anyone to actually walk up there added to the horror of the occasion.

There is also a spirit, dressed in pink and surrounded by a pink glow, called (fairly unimaginatively) the Pink Lady, who sometimes walks to the neighboring Church of the Holy Rude at Ladies' Rock. This elevated spot is where the damsels of the court watched their champions joust at tournaments. Some folks believe that this particular damsel is the sole survivor of Edward I's 1304 siege of the castle. Having escaped, it makes sense to these observers that she might return to find her husband killed in the siege. If that were the case, however, it might make more sense if she was actually entering the castle rather than leaving it.

Another of Stirling's phantom residents is a man, dressed in Highland garb, with kilt and all, who turns a corner and disappears into a door in the wall near the dungeon entrance. This would not be too disconcerting if the door in question had not been bricked up for decades! Enough people have seen this apparition to merit him mention on the old *Sightings* television show!

Stirling Castle
Castle Wynd
Stirling FK8 1EJ
United Kingdom

Tel: +44 (0) 1786 450000
Fax: +44 (0) 1786 464678
http://www.instirling.com/sight/castle.htm

The Skull in the Mirror

Castle Stuart was indeed built by a branch of the House of Stuart—but not by the royal family. Although the property did belong to the crown, there was no building on it when Mary Queen of Scots gave it to her illegitimate half-brother, James Stuart. Despite her love for him, and her granting him many favors (this land, the title of first earl of Moray, and occasional regency of the realm), he betrayed her, leading her opponents at the Battle of Langside to a victory that resulted in her exile and ultimate death.

James Stuart did not enjoy his ill-gotten gains for long; a disgruntled loyalist assassinated him. His son-in-law, the second earl of Moray, was also murdered by being stabbed thirteen times. But the third earl of Moray did finally complete Castle Stuart in 1625—only to see the property almost immediately seized and occupied by the MacIntosh clan, who had to be bribed in order to evacuate the place. After the Civil War, the castle became a neglected ruin, until at last the present owners, American members of yet another branch of the Stuart clan, restored the place after leasing it from the present Lord Moray. Having made Castle Stuart habitable again, the Stuarts now take in guests, who are warmly welcomed— even as they are told about the permanent residents.

The Stuarts were not the first to attempt to renew Castle Stuart. That honor may belong to a Canadian gentleman, one John Cameron, who tried to restore the castle back in the 1930s. He was so in love with the place that one night he continued to work long after his laborers had left. Up on a ladder, he discovered a section of plaster different in texture from the rest of the wall that sounded hollow when he knocked on it. Cameron decided that it must be the entrance to the sealed-off tower. His excavations exposed steps, and then his chisel broke through into an empty space. At that moment, he heard a voice scream "No!" All alone in the castle, he decided that it must have been his imagination, and worked on. As he aimed another blow, he felt a force push him in the chest, which caused him to fall backwards off the ladder. The smell of rot filled the room, and Cameron felt another presence there with him. He ran out of the building to the safety of his car.

But he knew he had to return. The temporary electric lights were still on, his tools and his flashlight were there, and he felt he could not stomach the ridicule he would face if his workmen found out a ghost had scared him away. Marshalling his resolve, Cameron turned the car lights on, so as to illuminate the room he would have to reenter when he turned off the house lights. He gingerly proceeded to the door and wedged it open, maintaining eye contact with the car's headlights at all times. All was quiet; his tools were there, and his flashlight, which he had broken in his haste to escape. Gathering it all up, he turned off the lights.

Instantly, the room was pitch-dark, with no sign of his headlights. Panicking, he felt his way to the door. It was closed, even though he had wedged it open! He then felt cold fingers grab him, and begin to pull him back toward his excavation. Cameron yanked himself free, rushed outside, and sped off in his car. He never returned to Castle Stuart. Nevertheless, restoration would eventually occur.

When the current operators began restoration, they included the long sealed-off East Tower. This structure had had a bad reputation for a long time, but the fact that the roof had been torn off in a storm in 1798 was what really forced its closure. Already, the three-turreted room at the top was called the "Haunted Room." One of the earls of Moray decided to return to Castle Stuart after a long sojourn in London. But the earl soon found that the screams and shrieks he heard during the night—although he saw nothing— were enough to convince him to move elsewhere.

Even so, His Lordship wanted to know what was making his home uninhabitable. He asked the dominie at Petty Parish Church to announce that the earl was offering a £20 reward (roughly $1,500 today) to anyone who could solve the mystery. Despite the poverty of the area, no one was quick to accept the challenge, so evil was Castle Stuart's reputation.

At last, four men took up the earl's offer: an elder of the Kirk, a shoemaker, an intrepid Highlander named Rob Angus, and the minister himself. It was agreed that each would spend one night alone in the Haunted Room, locked in from the outside. They would not compare notes about what befell them until each had completed his vigil. If their experiences revealed the room's secret and earned the earl's reward, they would split the money evenly.

The first night, it was agreed that the minister would spend the night. Although he went to sleep quickly, he had a dream in which an enormous Highland chief with bloodstained clothes came into the room and sat down next to his bed. The minister awoke, but saw nothing.

Next night, it was the turn of the Kirk elder (in the Scots Presbyterian Church, an elder is a member of the council which governs a parish). He stayed awake, reading his Bible. The Highland chief reentered the room after midnight. Drawing his dagger, he demanded to know what business the elder had there. That worthy man was too scared to answer, and fainted of fright; but before he did so, he stared up at the mirror over the fireplace and saw a grinning skull reflected back at him. He was never the same man again.

When the shoemaker took his turn, he resolved to spend it in prayer. But again, just after midnight, a tall, dark figure entered the room. The shoemaker also fainted as the thing drew up a chair and sat down next to him. He also reported seeing a skeleton in the mirror before he passed out.

We will never know, from this side of the grave, what happened to Rob Angus. When a servant opened the door to the room in the morning, the furniture was destroyed and the mirror smashed to bits. Angus was found outside the window, having fallen to his death. A few days later, a shepherd who had been passing by the night Angus died testified that around 12:30 A.M., he had heard fighting up in the tower room. He then saw Angus smash through the window and plummet to the ground. Looking up to the window, he saw the devil grinning back at him.

No major mishap seems to have occurred since the Stuarts reopened the whole of Castle Stuart, including the Haunted Room in the East Tower, which is also available for lodging. But people continue to report strange sounds and the feeling of being grabbed by cold fingers. If you stay there, perhaps you may discover what happened to Rob Angus.

Castle Stuart
Petty Parish, Inverness IV1 7IH
Scotland

Tel: +44 (0) 1463 790745
Fax: +44 (0) 1463 792604
http://www.castlestuart.com/
E-mail: castlestuart1625@btinternet.com

The Thing at Glamis

Lovers of Shakespeare will recall Glamis Castle as the setting of the foul murder of King Duncan in *Macbeth*. But a different castle with that name now stands on the spot, and it is likelier that the historical Macbeth defeated and killed Duncan in battle, rather than in his bed. But no matter, because the authentic story of Glamis is as strange as anything in fiction.

In 1372, King Robert II of Scots named Sir John Lyon the Thane of Glamis, granting him the site of the royal hunting lodge where Malcolm II had died in 1032. Four years later, Sir John married the king's daughter, Princess Joanna. Their descendants became the earls of Strathmore and Kinghorne in 1767. Thanks to a marriage, the name became Bowes-Lyon. Since the building of the current castle in 1400, successive generations have expanded and improved it, entertaining many royal guests along the way, such as Mary Queen of Scots and James VIII—son of the exiled James VII and father of Bonnie Prince Charlie—during his abortive attempt to regain the throne in 1715. At that time, James used the chapel for the mystical ceremony of "touching for the King's Evil," by which the legitimate kings of Great Britain cured scrofula by laying their hands on the sufferer.

It would be hard to overemphasize the importance of Glamis Castle in national life, especially as Her Late Majesty Queen Elizabeth the Queen Mother, parent of the current sovereign, was born here in 1899. She had a very happy childhood at the castle, apparently. But despite the recent status of Glamis as a happy family home, strange things walk there. Indeed, it claims the title of "most haunted castle in Scotland."

The initial haunting of the castle is claimed to date back to the time of Sir John himself, because of his removal of an ancestral chalice from the Lyon seat at Forteviot, where it was supposed to reside forever, much like the Luck of Muncaster. A Grey Lady haunts the chapel where James VIII called down heaven upon the diseased. She is rumored to be Lady Janet Douglas, who was burned at the stake as a witch on Castle Hill, Edinburgh, in 1537. Charged with plotting to poison King James V, her adherents have always claimed that the accusation was trumped up. Whether or not that is true, she has been seen several times recently (once by James Wentworth Day), both kneeling in the chapel and floating above the Clock Tower, wreathed in flames. When the Queen Mother was a little girl, she and her brother David (later to become earl himself) would put on gray cloaks and pretend to be her. To this day one corner pew is never occupied out of respect to her.

There is also a tongueless lady who both prowls the grounds and looks out at passersby from a barred window in the castle. Although no one has suggested her identity, she apparently derives great glee from pointing out her tongueless state to those who see her. Another ghost is a sickly-looking lady who peers out from a window halfway up the tower. Her face then vanishes, to be succeeded by bloodcurdling shrieks.

A few years ago, a well-known Edinburgh barrister drove to Glamis one evening for a dinner party. Driving into the grounds, he saw a figure apparently dressed in white. She glided along the ground, keeping pace with the car all the way to the doors, whereupon she vanished. As all the maids were indoors that night, it could not have been one of them. Given her speed and shadowy appearance, the barrister reluctantly concluded that he had seen a ghost.

By the door of the queen's bedroom, the ghost of a young African boy has been seen. A former servant who was ill treated two centuries back, the boy keeps his phantom vigil on a stone seat. When a servant girl—apparently a vampire—was caught drinking the life out of a fellow staff member, she was walled up alive—and she may be there yet! There is even a giant ghost clad in armor who occasionally appears to guests.

The portion of the roof called the "Mad Earl's Walk" is haunted during stormy weather, while disembodied swearing and stamping are heard from the abandoned tower. Whether or not it is securely locked, a door opens every night, while mysterious hammering sounds, knocking noises, and bedclothes being pulled off of guests are routine occurrences.

But by far the most notorious tales about Glamis Castle are those that feature the secret room. There are more windows visible from the outside at Glamis than can be reached from the interior, giving rise to immense speculation about a sealed room. In a place so old, and so filled with mystery and spirits, it would not be surprising to find that such a room—or rooms—exists. There are two very different stories about the chamber, which may well both be true if there are in fact *two* sealed rooms—something quite possible, given the size of Glamis Castle.

One cycle of tales centers around Alexander Lindsay, the fourth earl of Crawford, often called Earl Beardie in the stories, who died in 1454. A rebel against James II, he was a cruel and nasty man, liked by few except his friend, the earl of Glamis at the time. He is the one who is said to pace the Mad Earl's Walk, and may be the figure in armor. Crawford was renowned for his love of gambling. One Sunday night, while enjoying the Earl of Glamis's hospitality (and drinking heavily with him), he wandered about the castle demanding a partner for a card game. No one would break the Sunday observance this way, and so he went back to his room shouting that he would play with the devil himself. A tall man in dark clothes arrived at the castle and offered to play. They went into a room and began. The challenger was revealed as the devil, and so the room was bricked up. It is said that they (and a few of the earl's boon companions) are playing yet, and may be heard some nights doing so. Of course, His Lordship must get out now and then to keep his date on the Mad Earl's Walk.

But there is another less fanciful and more sinister tale about the sealed room of Glamis: that of the deformed twelfth earl. This sad story is said to have its beginning in 1821. At that time, a boy was born to the eleventh earl of Strathmore. What should have been a joyous event was a tragedy. The child had terrible defects: an egg-shaped body, tiny arms and legs, and no neck. Rather than expose the family to shame or scandal (in an age where deformed children were held to be the result of some nameless sin on the part of the parents, or at least the ancestors), word went out that the babe had died. But in reality, the boy lived, and was confined to a room whose windows were then bricked up. On dark and stormy nights, when it was unlikely that any servants (who were not in on the secret) would be around, the lad was exercised on the Mad Earl's Walk.

Then a second, perfectly healthy boy was born to the earl. When this child came of age at twenty-one, he was introduced to his confined brother. On the eleventh earl's death, the second son succeeded the firstborn, but the new earl was ever mindful of his brother as the rightful heir to the title. Despite his deformities, the older brother grew strong, and lived to be more than a hundred years old. Each heir was introduced to the confined brother when he reached his twenty-first birthday. Only three men were supposed to have known the secret at any one time: the current earl of Strathmore, the family lawyer, and the manager of the estate. Supposedly, a pictorial commemoration of the secret exists. This is a portrait showing the earl of Strathmore with his two sons and an indescribably deformed dwarf, whose skeleton is believed to be preserved somewhere in the castle.

At one time a Lady Strathmore approached the estate's broker, and asked him for the truth about the family secret. In a response worthy of Jack Nicholson in *A Few Good Men,* he replied, "It is fortunate you do not know the truth, for if you did you would never be happy." In 1904, the fourteenth earl of Strathmore, Claude Bowes-Lyon, told a friend, "If you could only know the nature of the terrible secret, you would go down on your knees and thank God it was not yours." He is also claimed to have told his daughter, Lady Mary Frances Bowes-Lyon, "You cannot be told; for no woman can ever know the secret of Glamis Castle."

It is rumored that various male members of the royal family know the secret of what was or is at Glamis. They, of course, are not talking. While you are unlikely to discover the truth of this particular story, should you visit the castle yourself, its phantom denizens may keep you busy!

The Castle Administrator
Estates Office
Glamis by Forfar
Angus DD8 1RJ
Scotland

Tel: +44 (0) 1307 840393
Fax: +44 (0) 1307 840733
http://www.glamis-castle.co.uk/

Two Ghostly Ladies

Crathes Castle sits upon lands that have been held by the Burnetts of Leys for centuries. Robert the Bruce granted the Burnetts this land in return for their support during the War of Independence against Edward I. The head of the family was made Royal Forester of Drum, with the celebrated Horn of Leys as his badge of office. The original home of the family was a house called Leys on an island in a nearby loch.

Their reason for abandoning the old but impregnable house for the secure location that is now Crathes was supernatural in origin. The laird of Ley at the time had died, leaving his son Alexander under the care of his domineering mother. Lady Agnes, as she was called, intended that her son should marry a daughter of one of the great noble houses. Instead, Alexander fell in love with a distant cousin, Bertha, who had been entrusted to them for a few months. Alexander was called away on business; Bertha began pining away. When the young man returned, it was to his beloved's deathbed.

As he stood by the corpse, his mother came to comfort him. He reached out to take a goblet of wine nearby—perhaps to share the last drink his love had tasted—when his mother grabbed it out of his hands, and threw it out the window. The young man realized that his mother had poisoned Bertha. A few months later, Bertha's father came to collect her, only to find out about her death. When Lady Agnes tried to explain the circumstances, the room turned chill. Alexander's mother screamed, pointed, and shrieked out, "She comes! She comes!" Lady Agnes then fell dead to the floor. Trying to escape his memories, Alexander built Crathes. On the anniversary of Bertha's death, however, a phantom crosses the country from the site of the old castle of Leys to Crathes. Some say it is Bertha, and others, Lady Agnes.

From that time on, the Burnetts settled in their new home and played a minor but important part in Scots history. Alexander married Janet Hamilton, and in 1563 he fought for Mary Queen of Scots at the Battle of Corrichie. Most of his successors were well regarded by the poor of the neighborhood. But another Alexander, the fourteenth laird and fourth baronet, earned the contempt of many for refusing to join either of the Jacobite Risings of 1715 and 1745. As the years went on, succeeding Burnetts made improvements to both house and gardens that are extremely visible today. In his youth, Sir Robert, eventually the eleventh baronet, emigrated to California in the nineteenth century. A very successful rancher, at one time he owned half of the city of Los Angeles. But post–World War II taxation did to the Burnetts what various armies could not. It drove them out of Crathes. In 1952, the thirteenth baronet gave Crathes Castle and a portion of the estate to the National Trust for Scotland, although the current laird and his family live in the House of Crathes, a short distance from the Castle.

Today the beautiful rooms of Crathes Castle are open to the public. Among these is the Green Lady's Room. It takes its name from a spirit who is said to be the ghost of a Burnett daughter. Back in the early eighteenth century, she became enamored of a servant and produced a child by him. He was dismissed, but the mother and her newborn simply vanished. No one knew where they had gone until the mid-nineteenth century, when workmen modernizing what is now the Green Lady's Room turned up the hearthstone in the fireplace. There they found the skeletons of an adult woman and newborn infant. At once an explanation was found for the seemingly overwhelming fear of ghosts the family members of a century before had evidently possessed. Although the remains were decently interred in the nearby churchyard, the Green Lady began to appear from this time forward.

Although today she is more often heard than seen, she does make appearances in the Green Lady Room, infant in arms, crossing the room only to vanish into the fireplace. Most often her appearances have been precursors of troubled times or even death for a member of the Burnett family. If you run into her at Crathes, you may feel grateful that you, at least, are not a member of the family!

Crathes Castle, Garden & Estate
Banchory, Aberdeenshire AB31 5QJ
Scotland

Tel: +44 (0) 1330 844525
Fax: +44 (0) 1330 844797
http://www.nts.org.uk/
E-mail: crathes@nts.org.uk

A Cursed Castle

uilt as a royal stronghold, Fyvie Castle was constructed by the Scottish Crown as one of a chain of fortresses throughout medieval Scotland. The first king in connection with this place is William the Lion, back in 1211. Located outside Turriff in Aberdeenshire, a royal forest surrounded the castle, where hunting was reserved to the king. Robert the Bruce himself held open-air court and dispensed justice under the beech trees of the forest. Long centuries later, the child who would become king played in these woods, although his father no longer owned them. The thirteenth century was certainly the royal heyday at Fyvie.

Not far away, at what is now called Earlston but in those days was Erceldoune, there lived an extraordinary man named Thomas. Thomas of Erceldoune—or "True Thomas," as some called him—was a very handsome poet. Now, a poet in those days was not merely a versifier, although "Thomas the Rhymer" was another nickname of the Bard of Erceldoune. Such men told stories or expounded upon history in their poems, and folks of all classes gathered to hear them—especially at a time when most could not read. Moreover, they had the ability, through their satires, to make or ruin reputations.

Near the town in which Thomas lived was a stream called Huntly Burn. On its bank, under a particular tree, the poet loved to lie down, to think and compose. One day, the queen of the fairies of the nearby Eildon Hills rode by on her milk-white horse. She wore green silk and velvet, and on her horse's mane were fifty-nine silver bells. At first he thought she was an apparition of the Virgin Mary, but she assured him that she was simply the queen of Elfland. The two were quite taken with each other, and she bore him away to her home, saying, according to the old ballad:

> Don't you see yon bonnie, bonnie road
> That lies across the ferny brae?
> That is the road to fair Elfland
> Where you and I this night must go.

For seven years he lived in her realm, and pleased her mightily. As a reward, she gave him the gift of prophecy. He was then returned to the world of men, on the proviso that he would return when she wanted him.

Back among his own kind he foretold many important events, such as the defeat of Mary Queen of Scots' forces at Langside in 1567, and the Union of the Crowns in 1603. Thomas wrote "Sir Tristrem," the oldest recorded Scots poem. One day he went back to the tree. Apparently his queen wanted him again; he vanished and was never seen again. Even so, as with Arthur, Charlemagne, and Frederick Barbarossa, it is claimed that he will come back when his country needs him most.

What concerns us here is that in the midst of his other activities, Thomas took the time to curse Fyvie Castle. The malediction stated that if three stones—taken from an ancient church and deposited in as many spots—were not gathered together, no direct heir would be born to the family who owned Fyvie. The curse has proven to be true. The "weeping stone," one of these three stones, is kept in the castle, underneath the Charter Room. Not only is it reported to weep water in the sight of the rightful heir, but legend has it that the heir will die and his wife go blind if they ever enter the room.

In the early seventeenth century, Sir Alexander Seton altered the old keep into the splendid Renaissance palace we see today. In 1984, its last private owner, Sir Andrew Forbes-Leith, sold the castle, its contents, and its gardens to the National Trust for Scotland. This gift to the nation included many. . . er. . . invisible assets as well. There is a resident Gray Lady, who did not make her initial appearance until the early 1900s. At that time, the lord of the castle noticed that one of the bedroom walls was covered with mold. Workmen called in to remove it discovered a secret room that contained a skeleton. No one knew who it was, but the owner gave it a decent burial. In a reverse of what usually happens when a body is properly put to rest, this is when the trouble began. The Gray Lady began appearing all over the castle, and mysterious sounds and poltergeist-like activity were the order of the day. Worn out by this treatment, the proprietor ordered the skeleton returned to its former place in the castle, and the room once again sealed up. The Gray Lady has not been seen since.

Another color-coded ghost who still walks is the Green Lady. She is always seen leaving the aptly named Haunted Chamber. She then glides noiselessly through the corridors and rooms of the castle before returning to the chamber from which she came and then vanishing. In life she was Lilies D. Drummond, wife to Sir Alexander, creator of the house we see today. However splendid a builder Sir Alexander was, he was not much of a husband. When another woman caught his fancy, he let his wife starve to death by not allowing her to be fed. The errant lord married his mistress, but as the alterations in the master bedroom were still being carried out, the pair had to spend their wedding night in a small, rarely used room.

That night, they heard soft, melancholy, disembodied sighs, but nothing else untoward. The next morning, however, there was a surprise awaiting them on the outside stone windowsill. Lilies D. Drummond's name was very precisely carved into the sill, with the letters each a few inches deep. With the technology that was available then, this would have taken a very long time to do. Moreover, the lettering is upside down, facing outside. The carver would have had to float or erect a scaffold outside and face inside the room, suspended several hundred feet in the air. Although this is now—and certainly was then—impossible, Lilies's name may be read there today. And, of course, she does make those occasional visits!

There is also a phantom trumpeter, who in life was a man named Andrew Lammie. In the eighteenth century, he fell in love with the local miller's daughter, one Agnes Smith. Her parents very strongly disapproved of the match. In this, the laird—who wanted Agnes as his mistress—seconded them. When he found out that the pair continued to meet secretly, he had Andrew kidnapped and sent as a slave to the West Indies. Lammie escaped a few years later, but when he returned he found out that Agnes had died shortly after his kidnapping. This revelation did little for his health, shattered as it had been in the sugar plantations. But Lammie swore before his death that the peal of a trumpet would sound just before the death of every future laird, to remind the family of the injustice he had suffered. So it happened for many years following. Sometimes a tall man in an expensive kilt and kit would be seen leaning against the castle wall, only to vanish when approached. This figure is generally identified as the wronged trumpeter.

Prior to the sale of the castle in 1984, being laird of Fyvie demanded a high tolerance for supernatural activity. The advice given by one such proprietor would be wise for present-day visitors to follow in such situations: "Do not try to combat the supernatural. Meet it without fear, and it will not harm you."

———————

Fyvie Castle
Fyvie, Turriff, Aberdeenshire AB53 8JS
Scotland

Tel: +44 (0) 1651 891266
Fax: +44 (0) 1651 891107
http://www.aboutbritain.com/FyvieCastle.htm

Emerald Isle—Haunted Isle

I f any country is a rival to Scotland for importance in the English-speaking diaspora, it is certainly Ireland. Saint Patrick's Day has, until recent years, been a far greater fete in New York, Boston, and Chicago than in Dublin. Irish music, Irish dancing, and Irish whiskey have been a great solace to the millions of descendants of exiles from Erin's Isle throughout the United States and the Commonwealth. As much as this heritage has been distorted through the lenses of nostalgia and stereotyping, the fact remains that Ireland even has a hold on the imagination of those who have never been there.

Two aspects of the Irish character in particular exercise this hold. The one is the age-old struggle between England and Ireland. Although, in one form or another, it has been ongoing since the twelfth-century Anglo-Norman invasion, the religious separation introduced by the success of the English Reformation irrevocably poisoned relations between the two peoples. The presence of the

Ulster Scots—Presbyterian settlers "planted" by James I to subdue rebellious Ulster—added an impediment which remains to this day in the form of their descendants, the Orangemen.

As a result of this history, there are several "generations" of castles and keeps in the Emerald Isle. Apart from the mounds left by the early Celts, pre-Celts, and Vikings, there are those ruins left by such Irish clans as the O'Neills, O'Briens, and O'Connors; the castles of Norman families like the Butlers and Fitzgeralds (any Irish family name starting with "Fitz-" is of Norman French origin—*Fils*Gerald, for example, meant "illegitimate son of Gerald"); and the residences of Anglo-Irish families who began settling in the country (and ruling the local scene) in the seventeenth century. Many of the homes of the latter (which, in turn, were often reworked versions of earlier castles left behind by the Irish or Normans) were burned out during the "Troubles" of 1919 to 1924. (A humorous and fictional account of one such happening is chronicled in Ray Bradbury's short story, "The Terrible Conflagration Up at the Place.")

The other, pleasanter aspect of the Irish mind is the mystical one. For, as with all Celtic peoples, the Irish traditionally went in for fairies and the like. The many stories of the leprechaun reveal this fascination. So, too, do their ghost stories, and there are few Irish castles that do not boast at least one spirit.

This author himself heard a ghostly choir sing in an old chapel in Athlone, an experience he will never forget. It is a country where, at least in its remoter spots, it seems as though anything could happen. Judging from the following tales, it does!

Within the Pale

There is no building more bound up with the course of Irish history than Dublin Castle. In appearance, it hardly looks like the typical idea of a castle. Except for one medieval-looking tower and the Gothic chapel, what you see is mostly an eighteenth-century construction in the graceful Georgian style for which Dublin is so famous. But do not be taken in by appearances. There has been a stronghold of some kind on these premises since Viking days. It was the Vikings, in fact, who first founded Dublin, as they did Cork and Waterford, Galway and Wexford. Prior to their coming, cities as such did not exist in Ireland; the pastoral population gathered around the hill-forts of their warrior kings, of which the most famous was certainly Tara, the seat of the High King.

But in 1171, the Anglo-Normans, who had been invited into the country as allies of one side in a civil war, set up in Dublin and decreed it their capital. The old Viking stronghold became the seat of their power, playing much the same role in Dublin as the Tower or Edinburgh Castle play in London and Scotland. The Pope made the king of England lord of Ireland as well, in order to end the continuous civil strife wracking the island. In the end, though, it made things worse. Many Anglo-Norman families came over from England and Wales and carved out fiefdoms for themselves. All the while, the lord lieutenant reigned from the castle as viceroy for the English king. But Ireland worked its magic on the Normans. Over the centuries the natives assimilated them, and the "Pale" (as the English area was called) gradually contracted back to the zone around Dublin. The area outside English control was literally "beyond the Pale."

This development would be reversed by Henry VIII; not only did he insist that all the Catholic churches within the Pale join his new Anglican church, he also aggressively sought to expand English control throughout the island. In 1541 he named himself "King of Ireland." From then on, bloody reprisal followed bloody rebellion. In 1688 King James II, perhaps the last man who could have reconciled the two countries equitably, was overthrown. From then on, Irish history followed its turbulent course down to the country's independence in 1922.

All of this meant a strange double life for Dublin Castle. On the one hand, as the seat of the viceregal court, from January to Saint Patrick's Day (the "Season"), the castle's lavish state apartments were filled with glittering social events such as balls, receptions, debuts, and state banquets. As the centuries wound on, the lord lieutenant's role became ever more purely ceremonial, with the chief secretary (who was also based in Dublin Castle) shouldering ever more of the burden of actual rule. As the headquarters of the British administration, the castle was the location of a prison and the focus of local hatred. During any of Ireland's successive rebellions, it was an inevitable target of attacks, as well as the center for their suppression. Orders to arrest those suspected of subversive activities would always come from the castle.

After independence, although various lesser branches of government continued to be housed in the castle complex, the focus of power moved elsewhere. Although he served as the king's representative under the Irish Free State, the governor-general had nothing to do with the place. Since 1937, the presidents of the Irish Republic are inaugurated there, and often host public events at the castle, but its role has become more symbolic. Its symbolism is, nevertheless, important, as it reflects who rules in Ireland. The chapel referred to earlier, for example, was the Anglican Chapel Royal until 1942. In that year it was consecrated as the Catholic Church of the Holy Trinity. In recent years, it has become a non-denominational chapel and art center, reflecting the secular mindset of Ireland's current rulership.

With such a history, one would expect Dublin Castle to be filled with ghosts. Oddly enough, it is not. What spirits are present reflect a very ordinary aspect of one particular episode. The British administration in Ireland kept the place filled with minor bureaucrats of all descriptions, in addition to those of the lord lieutenant's staff. Back in the mid-nineteenth century, one of the lord lieutenant's personal staff was working late, when two file clerks, dressed in the clothing of a half century before, passed through his office. Carrying papers, they ignored him—chatting all the while—and crossed through a door sealed up long ago. Since then, the pair have been seen by a number of employees at the castle. Once they were overheard speaking about Wolfe Tone, a leader of the nationalist agitation movement in the eighteenth century.

It is interesting that the ghosts of the castle are neither kings nor warriors, lords lieutenant nor nobles, but merely minor bureaucrats. Thus we may be assured that the absolutely essential element of government transcends time and space, and even the grave.

Dublin Castle
Dublin 2
Ireland

Tel: +353 (1) 677 7129
Fax: +353 (1) 679 7831
http://www.dublincastle.ie/
E-mail: info@dublincastle.ie

Young Churchill's Haunt

Phoenix Park in Dublin was laid out as a royal park in the eighteenth century, like Green or St. James's Park in London. A hunting ground, the deer in the park were held to belong to the king. As a result, it was thought entirely appropriate for the three major functionaries of British rule, whose headquarters were at Dublin Castle, to have country residences in what was then a remote district. The chief secretary was given a house in the park (now belonging to a U.S. ambassador) as was his under-secretary (currently belonging to the Papal Nuncio). During the 1780s, a private house in the park was bought for the lord lieutenant, and renamed Viceregal Lodge. The lodge became the viceroy's residence outside the "Season," when he moved back to Dublin Castle to preside over the capital's social life.

As the home of the Monarch's representative, Viceregal Lodge sometimes played host to the English royalty. Victoria, Edward VII, and George V all stayed there. But less pleasant events occurred there as well, as in 1881, when the chief secretary, Lord Frederick Cavendish, and the undersecretary, F. H. Burke, were stabbed to death with surgical knives. The perpetrators were members of a small terrorist group called the Invincibles. The pair had been walking back to the lodge from Dublin Castle, and their screams were heard from a ground-floor window by the lord lieutenant, the fifth Earl Spencer (who was an ancestor of Diana, the late Princess of Wales).

After independence in 1922, Viceregal Lodge became the residence of the governor-general of the Irish Free State. As with Canada or Australia today, the king remained head of state, although the government was completely separated from Great Britain. In 1932, however, a new governor-general, Domhnall Ua Buachalla, was installed in a hired private mansion in the south side of Dublin in order to escape the colonial overtones of Viceregal Lodge. These had apparently dissipated by 1938, when the first president of the Republic of Ireland, Douglas Hyde, moved in. Renamed Áras an Uachtaráin, it has served as the presidential residence ever since. As such, it has played host to innumerable celebrities and foreign heads of state.

Like Dublin Castle, the scene of so many exciting happenings ought to be more thoroughly haunted, but there is only one known ghost: a very small boy in Victorian dress who runs through the house. Apparently, he is very mischievous, and enjoys himself to no end. Those who have seen him (presidential staff, for the most part) say he looks like one boy and no other: young Winston Churchill. Churchill's grandfather, the Duke of Marlborough, was lord lieutenant from 1876 to 1880, when young Winston was between the ages of two and six. He stayed with his grandparents a good deal of the time, and in later years looked back to the era at Viceregal Lodge as the happiest time and place of his life. Apparently he still does. So it has come to pass that the part-Iroquois, half-American, former prime minister of Great Britain haunts the home of the president of Ireland. There is a moral here, it seems, but this author cannot figure out what it is!

Áras an Uachtaráin
Phoenix Park
Dublin 8
Ireland

Tel: +353 (1) 617 1000
Fax: +353 (1) 617 1001
http://www.irlgov.ie/aras/
E-mail: webmaster@aras.irlgov.ie

A Clutch of Phantoms

The first Saint Leger to come to Ireland was Anthony Saint Leger, dispatched by Henry VIII in 1537 to oversee the dissolution of monasteries in the area under English control. As a result of the wars of Henry and Elizabeth, large portions of the province of Munster came under English control. In those days, the area around Doneraile was under the control of the Synan clan, a Welsh family whose ancestors had come over with the Normans in the twelfth century.

The Synans sold Doneraile to Sir William Saint Leger in 1636. As lord president of Munster (the local representative of the king), he required a residence in keeping with his lofty status. Doneraile Castle became the seat of local government. The civil war between the king and parliament (1640–1645) that convulsed all three kingdoms of England, Scotland, and Ireland finally reached Doneraile. In Ireland, things were particularly confused, because there were not two but three parties playing against one another: the

Roundheads of Cromwell (who had much support among the Ulster Scots), the Anglo-Irish supporters of the king, and the "Old English" (still-Catholic Norman descendants and Gaels of the Confederacy of Kilkenny).

The latter group rose in rebellion against the English in 1641, and Sir William fought against them successfully. But he died the next year, and the rebels took Doneraile and plundered it. Rebuilt by Sir William's son in the 1660s, thirty years later his grandson, Arthur, began to build the present house that is now Doneraile Court.

Created Viscount Doneraile in 1703, Arthur had an unusually inquisitive daughter, Elizabeth. One afternoon in 1712, she had settled herself to read in a nook in her father's office. Behind some curtains, she was invisible to anyone who might be in the room. A group of men entered, among the voices of which she discerned her father's voice. She soon realized that they were holding a Masonic meeting. She was much frightened, since no non-member was allowed to listen in. She remained undiscovered until the meeting broke up, when her father's valet found her. Denouncing her to Lord Doneraile and his friends, he presented them with a problem. By their oaths, they were bound to kill any non-Mason who discovered lodge secrets by stabbing, beheading, hanging, or shooting. This prospect did not please any of them, but then Lord Doneraile had an idea. They would initiate her into the Masonic Order. And so they did. Elizabeth became the first (and only) female Mason in Ireland.

The eighteenth and nineteenth centuries were truly Doneraile's heyday. Not only was Doneraile Court finished, but the extensive gardens and the deer park were designed. One member of the family, Barry Saint Leger, served in the king's forces in America during the revolution there. Defeated by the rebel forces at Oriskany, he was prevented from linking up with General Burgoyne, thus paving the way for the British defeat at

Saratoga, the entrance of France into the war, and the creation of the United States.

But as was the case with so many families, the Saint Legers received their own supernatural harbinger of death. Coming out of the Canal Gate of the estate, a black coach drawn by four horses would tear down the driveway and off in the direction of Doneraile village whenever a Saint Leger was going to die. What made this sight even more impressive was that all four horses were headless! On a much talked-about occasion, in 1887, a passing farmer saw the coach, only to learn that the fourth Viscount Doneraile had died in the night.

The fifth viscount had only one daughter—Claire Saint Leger. A noted beauty, she married Lord Castletown and brought the estate with her as part of her dowry, while the title went to a cousin. The Castletowns entertained regularly, and their parties often included such luminaries as the Prince of Wales (later Edward VII). Even though she was fifteen years younger than he, Lady Castletown died earlier than her lord. He spent his remaining years in mourning, although he was able, during the Troubles, to convince the local IRA to not burn the place down.

In time, a divorce settlement took Doneraile out of family hands. Much neglected, it came at last into the possession of the Irish State, who has restored the grounds, while the Irish Georgian Society looks after the house and outbuildings. The grounds today include the deer park, inhabited by a herd of red deer first introduced in 1895. Although hunting has been strictly forbidden for decades, human law apparently does not impress the long-dead second Viscount Doneraile. One night in the 1990s, a gamekeeper at Doneraile Park and his son were making their rounds. They suddenly heard the baying of hounds. The only explanation they could think of was the possibility that the Doneraile pack, kept in kennels over a mile away, might have somehow escaped. But with the gates to the park locked, there was no way that this could have happened.

Just then, a pack of hounds emerged out of the shadows. After it passed them, a phantom rider in a broad-brimmed hat galloped after them. The cry of the hounds and the clatter of the horse's hooves seemed oddly muffled, and the face of the rider resembled pictures of the second viscount. The rider and the dogs swept around a bend in the avenue, and were lost to sight. Although there was no trace of either rider or hounds the next morning, other employees have reported seeing them from time to time.

A less energetic wraith is that of Lord Castletown himself, who has often appeared to visitors, in various rooms, always looking rather unhappy. His lady has appeared but once, to her niece, Geraldine Saint Leger. While looking through her aunt's room one day, years after her death, Miss Saint Leger stopped to look into the mirror. There she saw not her own face, but Lady Castletown's! At such a place as Doneraile Court, the term "family heirloom" can have a sinister ring. But who knows? The ghosts of the place might well enjoy some out-of-town company now and then.

Doneraile Forest Park
Doneraile
County Cork
Ireland

Tel: + 353 (0) 222 4244
http://homepages.iol.ie/ ~ nodonnel/forestpark.htm

Whimsical Hauntings

Castle Leslie stands by a lake near Glaslough, very close to the border of Northern Ireland. The Leslies were a Scots family. The first to come to Ireland was John Leslie, Anglican bishop of the Isles of Scotland, who, in June of 1633, was transferred to the diocese of Raphoe in Donegal. Called the "fighting bishop," he defeated Cromwell's forces at the Battle of Raphoe. When Charles II was restored, Bishop Leslie, at age ninety, rode from Chester to London in twenty-four hours. Five years later, the bishop bought Glaslough Castle and Demesne, only to die at the age of one hundred in 1671. Castle Leslie was now in the hands of the family who have owned it ever since.

The Leslies were Jacobites, and were friends of Jonathan Swift (who often stayed at Castle Leslie). Unusual for Anglo-Irish gentry, they were both friendly to Catholicism and well regarded by their tenants. In later years they tended to buck the establishment they belonged to, and back the more moderate wing of Irish nationalism. During the Great Famine, the Leslies did their best to alleviate the starvation all around them, employing many on make-work jobs and distributing free food to the neighborhood.

Sir John Leslie, the first baronet, was a painter. He and his wife, Constance, moved to Manchester Square in London, where he died in 1916. Lady Constance died in London on the same date, nine years later; but on the day of her death she was seen walking around Castle Leslie.

Upon his father's death, Sir John, the second baronet, inherited Castle Leslie. He had married Leonie Jerome, whose older sister Jenny married Lord Randolph Churchill. Thus, his children were first cousins to the future prime minister (whose ghost we have just met).

Sir John's oldest son, Shane, became an Irish Nationalist and converted to Catholicism. He also married an American, Marjorie Ide. In 1914, Sir John's second son, Norman, was killed while leading an assault on an enemy trench in World War I. He appeared on the terrace in broad daylight, one week before he was killed. He appeared standing next to a chest of drawers in the castle's red bedroom a few weeks after his death to his sister-in-law, Marjorie. Appearing in a cloud of light, he searched through his letters, as though he were looking for one especially. Marjorie sat up in her bed, saying, "Why, Norman—what are you doing here?" He turned to her and smiled. Then both he and the light faded away.

In 1943, Sir John's wife Leonie lay on her deathbed, attended by nurses around the clock. The night she died, an elderly woman entered the room and approached the dying woman. Speaking to her briefly, the aged visitor then left. Thinking it was a family member, the nurse said nothing, and shortly thereafter Leonie died peacefully in her sleep. After the funeral, as the family sat in the dining room, the nurse pointed out the lady in the portrait to the left of the fireplace as the one who had visited Leonie on her deathbed. It was Lady Constance, who, as we just saw, visited the castle shortly after her own death.

Sir Shane then inherited both the baronetcy and Castle Leslie. Among his works are *The Ghost Book of Sir Shane Leslie,* which is both an inquiry into the topic from the Catholic viewpoint and a collection of eerie tales. His wife, Lady Marjorie, died in 1951, and true to what has become a tradition for twentieth-century Leslie women, reappeared shortly after her death. At the moment of her death, she appeared in her son Desmond's London flat, where his own little boy, Sean, was dying. She touched her grandson and vanished. Sean then said, "Pain gone," and was suddenly completely cured of his illness.

Shortly afterwards, Desmond's mother-in-law, Emmy, had a sort of vision. Emmy saw Marjorie pointing across the lake on the Castle Leslie property to a fantastic palace glowing in the sky, saying, "Look where I am going to live now."

The haunted room at Castle Leslie boasts a haunted bed from Brede Place, a former home of the Leslies in Sussex, near Hastings. Brede was a leading contender for the title of "most haunted house in England," and the four-poster bed from 1607 does its best to carry on the tradition. Those who spend the night in the room often find that the doors open and close of their own accord. The bed has been known to levitate, and the mattress will push up or suddenly sink down. Sir John (Sir Shane's son and the current baronet) refuses to sleep there.

Castle Leslie is an intriguing place. It is open to the public and accepts overnight guests. Sir John's niece, Samantha, now runs it. This author has visited few more pleasant places in the whole of Ireland. But it stands as a reminder that ghosts can appear in even the pleasantest, most jovial of families.

Castle Leslie
Glaslough, County Monaghan, Ireland

Tel: + 353 47 88109
Fax: + 353 47 88256
http://www.castleleslie.com
E-mail: info@castleleslie.com

Ambiguous Haunts

The area around today's Ardgillan Castle was, in Gaelic times, the home of the O'Casey family. It later passed to the Talbot Earl of Tyrconnell. But the disruption of Ireland in the seventeenth century saw Ardgillan pass through several hands. In 1737, it was acquired by the Reverend Robert Taylor. The following year, he began building the present house. Called a castle, Ardgillan is really just a large country-style house with castellated embellishments, such as decorative battlements added to the roof. The reverend originally named the house "Prospect." In addition to the central section, the west and east wings were added in the late 1700s.

Ardgillan remained the Taylor family home (later changed to Taylour) for two hundred more years. In 1962 the family sold the estate to a German gentleman, Heinrich Pott. In 1982 the Dublin County Council purchased Ardgillan Demesne, and it is now managed by Fingal Council.

Ardgillan became a regional park in June 1985. Interesting as the house undoubtedly is, the acres of gardens are what attract the public's major interest. Each of the different sections has a different horticultural theme, the most extraordinary of which is the Yew Walk. Planted in 1800s under the supervision of Marianne Taylor, wife of Reverend Henry Edward Taylor, it was the favorite walk of Captain Edward Taylour. But folks disagree about the identity of the indiscriminate, shadowy form occasionally seen here; is it Marianne or Edward?

The gender of the spirit that lurks on the "Lady Bridge"—the pedestrian footbridge running above the Balbriggan–Skerries Road and the Dublin–Belfast Railway Line, along the northeastern boundary of the park—is not in doubt, however. As the bridge's name suggests, a spectral lady dressed in white has often been seen crossing this bridge. Witnesses usually experience a deep chill upon seeing the figure. Although this "Lady in White" is also seen in the castle itself, if anyone speaks to her, she disappears. Opinions differ as to which Taylour she is, but all agree that she must be a member of the family.

While explanations for and identification of the spirits in this house may vary, all presume they spring from the ranks of the Taylour family. This is the problem with selling an ancestral home: You may leave someone behind!

Ardgillan Castle
Balbriggan, County Dublin
Ireland

Tel: + 353 (1) 849 2212
Fax: + 353 (1) 849 2786
http://www.iol.ie/ ~ cybmanmc/index.htm
E-mail: cybmanmc@iol.ie

Haunted Holidays

James Shaw, a native of Greenock, Scotland, built Ballygally Castle in 1625. He had come to Ireland, as so many of his countrymen did, to seek his fortune in 1606. He arrived in the Ballygally area of County Antrim in 1613, and purchased land from the earl of Antrim. It was on this property that Ballygally Castle was built in 1625. Soon after he married Isabella Brisbane, he placed over the main entrance door to the castle the following inscription: 1625—GOD IS PROVIDENS IS MY INHERITANS. Over this legend is a shield with the coats of arms of the Shaw and Brisbane families and their initials, J. S. and I. B.

The castle was used as a refuge for the Protestants during the civil wars. During the rebellion of 1641, the Irish garrison tried unsuccessfully to seize the place. Toward the middle of the eighteenth century, Henry Shaw made considerable additions to Ballygally after marrying a Miss Hamilton. Her two sisters (one a Mrs. Nixon) came to live at the castle. But in the early 1800s the Shaw family lost their lands and wealth, and Ballygally was sold to the Agnew family for £15,400. It was then sold to a succession of private owners, and at last to the Hastings Hotel Group in 1966, remaining in their possession ever since.

But these sales did not remove those former residents who decided to linger on. Although James Shaw thought enough of his wife to commemorate her on the door inscription, they did not get on well. When Isabella at last produced an heir, James took the baby from his wife and locked her in a room at the top of the castle. Attempting to escape from her prison, she fell out of a window to her death—although some say she had help. This unfortunate demise did not ruin her disposition, apparently. Over the years, many guests have encountered her in the halls, and even in their rooms. Despite her ill treatment, those who have met her consider her a friendly ghost.

In a corner turret of the tower is the Haunted Room, inhabited by Henry Shaw's sister-in-law. After her death, Mrs. Nixon haunted the castle, wandering around the corridors in a silk dress and knocking on doors. She still does this, although the management today often attributes these hallway visitations to Lady Isabella. But no one disputes the fact that she is the one who appears to guests in the Haunted Room.

There are a number of resident ghosts at Ballygally, and sometimes they appear as a group. Some years ago, an elderly couple checked in around Christmas for several days. When they arrived, they found staff members busy preparing for a costume ball. That night, one of the employees, clad in old-time clothes, knocked at their door and invited them down to the ball. The old couple went down and found staff and guests all in period costume. They had a wonderful time, and at last went up to bed. The next morning, over breakfast, they thanked the manager for such a wonderful time, and went on about how much they had enjoyed themselves. This left the manager a bit confused, as the ball was not scheduled for another two nights! The couple left hurriedly, and another chapter of mystery was added to the castle's chronicles.

It is really rather amazing, given the nature of hauntings, that so many occur here. Still, while one cannot guarantee that guests here will experience anything out of the ordinary, it is tempting to stay in a hotel where the room service includes echoes from beyond!

Coast Road, Ballygally
County Antrim BT40 2QZ

Tel: +44 (0) 28 2858 1066
Fax: +44 (0) 28 2858 3681
http://www.hastingshotels.com/hotel_ballygally_castle.html
E-mail: res@bgc.hastingshotels.com

Spectral Home and Garden

reland's most ancient oak woods surround Charleville Forest Castle. A druid center, the land was later occupied by a monastery until the time of Elizabeth I, when the city fathers of Dublin felt that its occupation was necessary as a security measure. In 1620, the lands of the O'Molloys around Tullamore were given to Sir John Moore. His descendant became the first lord of Tullamore in 1716, and was in turn succeeded by his son Charles. He became the first earl of Charleville in 1757, taking his title from the house in the woods to which he had relocated. Dying without children, his land passed to his nephew, John Bury.

It was John's son, Charles, who was also given the title of earl of Charleville, and who built the modern Charleville Forest Castle, naming it after the surrounding woods. As a leading Freemason and antiquarian, it is alleged that all sorts of esoteric considerations influenced his plans for the new building. Whether or not that is true, the castle has come to be known as "the scariest place in Ireland." It certainly is one of Ireland's most beautiful, and an important example of Gothic revival architecture.

Unfortunately, the castle was uninhabited after 1912, and roofless by 1968. But two ladies acquired the place and began the ongoing restoration. Now overnight visitors see luminous balls of ghostly light throughout the building, and the ghost of Charles Bury, first earl of Charleville, in one of the towers. There is also a young girl named Harriet who fell down some stairs to her death in the early 1800s. One employee declares that she heard the girl and other ghosts "in rooms above, moving furniture around and laughing and talking." Others have heard the sounds of children enjoying a game in what was once the nursery.

When Harriet appears on the great, winding staircase, wearing a shimmering blue chiffon dress, the temperature drops. On the stairs and the landing below, people often see her, skipping playfully in front of them. Sometimes the ghost of a small boy joins her. Once, the three-year-old son of one of the current owners went missing. The family eventually found him at the bottom of the stairwell, where he eagerly told of how "the little boy and girl" had looked after him as he came down the stairs.

On another occasion, after a party at the castle, a guest laid his bedroll on the floor and prepared to sleep. As he was nodding off, two elderly Englishmen began drinking and chatting excitedly with each other. Although he could hear them close at hand, they were invisible!

The current owner, Bonnie Vance, was awoken in her tower bedroom one morning around 3:00 A.M. She saw the first earl and Masterton, his architect, leading a ghostly procession around the room. It was comprised of a woman in a black hood, a little girl, and a group of about seventeen "monks or druids." They encircled her bed and, she believed, appeared to bestow a blessing upon her. Bonnie took this as a mark of approval on her restoration work.

The grounds harbor their own tales of the bizarre as well. In the park is the huge "King Oak," whose size bespeaks its great age. Whenever one of its branches fell, it was traditionally claimed to be a sign that a member of the Charleville family would die. In May of 1963, a huge bolt of lightning smashed into it, shattering its trunk from top to bottom. Although the oak survived, two weeks later, Colonel Charles Howard-Bury, last of the line to own Charleville Forest Castle, suddenly dropped dead.

The castle has a lot to offer in the way of architecture and scenery. Obviously, some have been unable to tear themselves away. Doubtless they are waiting to meet you!

Charleville Castle
Tullamore, County Offaly
Ireland

Tel: + 353 0506 21279
Fax: + 353 0506 23039
http://www.charlevillecastle.com/
E-mail: info@charlevillecastle.com

Blood and Stench

Leap Castle (*Leam Ui Bhanain*) was the principal seat of the O'Carrolls of Ely, guarding as it does a strategic pass through the Slieve Bloom Mountains. Rather a bloodthirsty bunch, the O'Carrolls were the last remaining clan of the area to surrender to the crown. This ferocity toward outsiders was not too surprising, given how they dealt with their own. When the Mulrooney, the chief of the clan, died in 1532, he left two sons. One day, one of the sons—a priest—offered Mass at the altar of the chapel over the main hall in the original tower. His brother, "one-eyed Tadhg," entered the chapel and slashed him to death with an ax. The room has been called the "Bloody Chapel" ever since. To seal his leadership, Tadhg O'Carroll of the Leap invited the members of a rural branch of his clan to a lavish banquet. No sooner were they seated than he ordered his servants to murder each of his guests.

The dungeon was notorious in its day for its implements of torture—racks, iron maidens, and the like. When an unhappy victim expired at last, his corpse was dumped down a drop door into an *oubliette*, a room where the unwanted were discarded. In time, the victim was forgotten, as the name implies. . . but the bones remained.

In 1599, Charles O'Carroll—who, as it would turn out, was to be the last ruling chieftain—hired some of the MacMahons of Monaghan to fight for him as mercenaries against the O'Neill Earl of Tyrone. When they were finished, O'Carroll got them dead drunk at a lavish feast, and had them all massacred in their sleep.

But the time of the O'Carrolls would soon come to an end. Charles O'Carroll continued the struggle against the English, capturing one of Cromwell's men, a Captain Darby from Leicestershire. Held prisoner in the castle dungeons, Darby made the acquaintance of his captor's daughter, who began smuggling food to him and finally arranged his escape. As the would-be fugitives made their way down the staircase, her brother confronted them. Darby ran him through and they escaped.

When they married in 1659, the castle passed into his hands. But Darby had certainly married into a (for him) congenial family. Assisted by two servants, he buried his treasures on the castle grounds. He then had these two servants murdered. As one of Cromwell's officers after Charles II was restored, he spent many years in prison for treason. When released, he could not remember where the hoard was hidden.

Not surprisingly, Leap Castle acquired a reputation for the supernatural. The Darbys' guests frequently were confronted by a tall female figure in a red gown who clutched a shining dagger in her hand.

Mildred Darby, wife of Jonathan Charles Darby (who had inherited the castle in 1880), made things even worse. She decided to hold a series of séances at the castle. In 1909, she wrote an account for the *Occult Review* of these gatherings, and the resultant activities of what she believed to be an elemental (a sort of non-human spirit). Mildred described how she was "standing in the Gallery looking down at the main floor, when I felt somebody put a hand on my shoulder. The thing was the size of a sheep. Thin, gaunt and shadowy. . . its eyes which seemed half decomposed in black cavities stared into mine. The horrible smell. . . gave me a deadly nausea. It was the smell of a decomposing corpse." Apparently, other such unpleasant entities began acting up at the same time.

Despite their unwelcome visitors, the Darbys stayed on at Leap Castle until 1922, when it was burned and looted during the Troubles. Following this event, the workmen who were gutting the interior found the long-forgotten oubliette behind a wall of the Bloody Chapel. Three cartloads of human bones were eventually removed from this little corner of hell.

The ruins acquired a frightening reputation among the local folk. The window of the Bloody Chapel would suddenly light up, as though lit for Mass. The lady in red who had frightened so many during the Darbys' sojourn was apparently unconcerned with the ruined state of her home—she was quite happy still to frighten wayfarers who walked at night among the ruins.

But in 1972 the castle was bought by an Australian of Irish descent, who in turn sold it to musician Sean Ryan and his wife, Anne, in 1991. They set about restoring the ruin into a livable home. However, mysterious accidents—one that left Sean with a fractured knee, and another with a broken ankle—plagued their efforts. Nonetheless, they persevered, and in time their work was done. The pair opened their home for tours and occasional musical evenings.

At first it seemed that the malevolence of the ghostly inhabitants had disappeared. But both the Lady in Red and the foul-smelling thing soon returned, and are occasionally seen. Sometimes new phantom boarders show up, as in May 2002, when Sean found a ghostly old man seated in a chair by a downstairs fireplace. Accustomed to such visitations by now, he simply wished the spirit "Good day" and went on about his business.

Should you find yourself among them, you may not feel as blasé about the otherworldly inhabitants of the castle as its owners do. But then, you do not have to live with them full-time!

Leap Castle
Roscrea, County Tipperary
Ireland

Tel: +353 (0) 509 31115

Puck's Return

Malahide Castle, near Dublin, was the home of the Talbot family for eight centuries. Since 1171, thirty individual Talbots have ruled there, starting with the first lord, Richard Talbot, who died in 1193, to the Honorable Rose Maude Talbot, who now lives in Tasmania. Her brother, Lord Milo Talbot de Malahide, died in 1973. So severe were the death duties (inheritance taxes) that the Irish Tax Board were able to accomplish something the British Crown could not—expel the Catholic Talbots from their home. The castle and its 268-acre demesne were purchased by Dublin County Council.

During the Middle Ages, successive Talbots aided the English king by defending the Pale from marauding Irish. But as the fifteenth century came on, these Norman paladins were rapidly assimilated, "becoming more Irish than the Irish themselves." When Cromwell seized Malahide, he banished the Talbots to Connaught and gave the castle to one Miles Corbet. During the restoration of Charles II, the castle was restored to the family. Through various scrapes, the family managed to hold on to Malahide. One member of the family was the priest who received Charles II into the Catholic Church on his deathbed. But once, their luck very nearly failed them. On the morning of July 12, 1690, fourteen male members of the clan sat down to breakfast, prior to joining James II at the Battle of the Boyne. Not one survived to nightfall. This would be their greatest defeat prior to that suffered at the hands of the taxman.

As we have come to expect, all of this history has given rise to hauntings. One of the best known is the ghost of a dwarf caretaker, suitably nicknamed "Puck." Despite being merely four feet tall, Puck possessed a heavy beard. His major job was to keep watch and sound the alarm in case Malahide was attacked. Living in a turret of the castle, subsequently called Puck's Staircase, he carried out his duties as watchman in a most exemplary manner. Keeping his room spotless, he was a bit of a recluse. His dinner would be left outside his door each night at sundown, and the next morning the empty trays and plates would be in the same spot. But one day, presumably tired of ridicule, he hanged himself from the Minstrel's Gallery, which overlooked the Great Hall.

Puck's ghost has appeared many times since. He has appeared in photographs taken in the Great Hall, easily recognizable by his height and beard. Photographs of the castle exterior have shown his face peering through the ivy covering of his turret. In many Talbot family letters, his periodic returns are mentioned. The last time he was seen was after the death of Lord Milo. A member of Sotheby's staff sat in the Great Hall, itemizing material for a forthcoming auction. Puck appeared on his staircase in front of the shocked worker, who had no prior knowledge of him, but gave a description that matched all the others exactly.

There are other ghosts at Malahide. Sir Walter Hussey, son of the baron of Galtrim, makes an appearance from time to time. In the fifteenth century he was killed in battle on the day of his wedding. Sir Walter wanders about the castle at night, pointing to the spear wound in his side and groaning horribly. Apparently he is annoyed at his bride, Lady Maud Plunkett, who after his death rushed to marry his rival, Lord Talbot de Malahide.

Lady Maud also appears—not as a fresh bride, but as she looked when she was married to her third husband, a lord chief justice. She had become a shrew by this time, and is seen chasing her hapless judicial mate throughout the castle.

The picture of a beautiful lady which has graced the Great Hall for years is unusual in that no one knows who the subject is. Even more unusual are her occasional jaunts, when she leaves her painting to wander through the castle at night. Seen by many people over a number of years, she is called simply the "White Lady."

The carved chimneypiece in the Oak Room of the castle depicts the coronation of the Virgin Mary as Queen of Heaven—a Catholic image if ever there was one. When Miles Corbet occupied Malahide Castle (thanks to Cromwell), the figure of the Virgin vanished from the chimneypiece. Remaining blank until Corbet's departure, the space was miraculously refilled by the Virgin, where she may be seen today.

Corbet was not a nice man, but he did have a conscience. Feeling guilty over having signed Charles I's death warrant, he would combat the resulting insomnia by riding a gray horse around the castle grounds. The area known as the Back Road today was once known as Corbet's Ride. Every April 19, the anniversary of Corbet's death, he can be heard galloping on his steed.

But Corbet also puts in an occasional appearance at the castle. When Charles II was restored, Corbet had to return his ill-gotten property (including Malahide) and suffer judgment for the many crimes he had committed—including the murder of Charles I and the desecration of the abbey near the castle. Hanged, drawn, and quartered, when his ghost appears, it seems at first to be a perfectly whole soldier in armor. It then falls into four pieces in front of the viewer's eyes.

Many other spirits may be found in the house and park. There is a field elsewhere on the grounds called Our Lady's Acre. Now and then, the translucent ghosts of two gray-haired, sad-faced ladies have been seen, wandering about aimlessly. No one seems to know who they are, like so many other hauntings at Malahide. Perhaps they will tell you!

Malahide Castle
Malahide, County Dublin
Ireland

Tel: +353 (1) 846 2184
Fax: +353 (1) 846 2537
http://www.malahidecastle.com

Ghosts of the Mother Continent

We Americans tend to forget that, for most of us, Europe is home. This might be obvious, considering what we have said about the influence of England, Scotland, and Ireland in the United States. But most Americans have roots in the Continent itself, be they Latin, Germanic, or Slavic. Unlike our cousins who stayed home, we Americans (unless we are Native Americans) cannot stand on a piece of our national real estate and say, "People of my blood stood here a thousand years ago." Europeans can. The history that produced us, from the Greek philosophers to 1492, is almost exclusively European history.

This history produced many conflicts, and so, as a result, many castles. It also produced innumerable able rulers, and so, many palaces. Very many of these boast hauntings, but as we shall see, accounts are generally not as detailed as in English-speaking lands. I suspect two reasons for this: Europeans tend to be more reluctant to admit to having experienced such things, and simultaneously, more blasé about them.

On the one hand, the first reaction might be linked to the Continent's rampant materialism; the second, however, may be part of the all-encompassing nature of European folklore. Many a European may not believe in God, but he will neither question nor affirm the existence of the "White Lady" in the local castle, or even that a nearby hill's origin lies in a clump of earth the devil dropped when accosted by the town's patron saint.

Thus, accounts of hauntings are often folkloric in nature. You will be solemnly told that the thing in the parlor appears regularly, but no one will admit to actually having seen it. We are a long way here from the psychical research so popular in Britain and America. That having been said, although your informer may tell you of the tradition regarding the ghost in a jocular manner, you are likely to get a cold stare if you pooh-pooh it yourself.

Another element in Catholic countries is the omnipresence of the Church. European believers tend to see ghosts in more theological terms than we do in the United States. Unsurprisingly, what could have been the site of a truly spectacular haunting was very purposefully destroyed. Mayerling, the Austrian hunting lodge where that country's Crown Prince Rudolf pulled off a successful double-suicide with his mistress back in the nineteenth century, would no doubt have been a ghostly happy hunting ground. But the prince's father, Emperor Franz Josef, had the place turned into a Carmelite convent. Now the place echoes with prayer rather than groans.

At the same time, Europeans are rather more given to celebration of the supernatural than we are. We have Hallowe'en, to be sure, but they have a number of such days. The nights of February 1 (Candlemas Eve), April 24 (Saint Mark's Eve), April 30 (May Eve, Walpurgis Nacht), June 23 (Saint John's Eve, Midsummer Eve), and July 31 (Lammas Eve) are celebrated in many locales with bonfires, fortune-telling rites, and tales of ghosts, witches, and fairies. Hallowe'en itself ushers in a sort of Triduum, with thoughts and prayers regarding the dead extending into All

Saints' and All Souls' days. In regions as diverse as rural France and Estonia, the whole month of November is considered a time when the dead return to their old haunts. . . or homes. These are times when religion and folklore mingle; although many might jump the bonfire, say, as a joke, they would, in their heart of hearts, be too afraid to discontinue the custom.

Both castles and bonfires have this in common: they offer safety. This is an important thing to understand about European weird lore, because so much of it derives from our ancestors' fear of the enormous forests that then surrounded their little villages. There were fearful inhabitants in them. Most fearsome of all, perhaps, was the *aurochs*, or wild bull. Ancestor of our modern cattle, it was a large black animal standing six feet at the shoulder with spreading, forwardly curved horns.

Just as fearsome was the European bison, forest-dwelling cousin of our own American buffalo. Somewhat resembling our version, it too could be found throughout the European forest. Much smaller but nastier in disposition was the wild boar. Hunted with spears, it had a cunning that was lacking in the larger bovines. The great hulking brown bear was smarter yet. There were the moose, which Europeans call elk, the red deer, the roe deer, and the fallow deer. Lesser game such as the genet, marten, fox, otter, badger, hare, rabbit, and squirrel were also present. Nor were beasts of prey absent either—the lynx and wildcat prowled. But perhaps dominant in our ancestors' minds was the wolf.

But other animals, less easily dealt with, also lived in the forest, as our ancestors believed: the unicorn, for one, and the dragon. Moreover, the fairies and rather more unpleasant characters in the way of goblins and demons could be found there also. While holy hermits might take up their residence in the forest's depths, so too might robbers—and not always benevolent ones like Robin Hood and his Merry Men, all under the merry greenwood tree. There too was the mysterious Green Man, a half-human, half-supernatural figure analogous in European folklore to the North American Indian Sasquatch or Bigfoot, and the Tibetan yeti. Those jungle-like woods of yesteryear are for the most part long gone; but their shadow remains on the European imagination. It is a shadow technology has only partly dispelled. Moreover, it is one unshared for the most part by their American cousins, who were able to subdue the natural world of their new continent in less than two centuries.

A familiar pattern in the hauntings is one we have already gleaned from the countries of the British Isles: the prevalence in castles and palaces of female spirits dressed in varying shades. After a while, it may seem a tad repetitive. In fact, no less a ghost hunter in the home of the nobility than HRH Prince Andrew of Greece himself, in his *Living with Ghosts*, declared in a slightly acidic tone: "I was fed up with the procession of White, Blue, Green, Red, and Black Ladies, one-legged, one-armed, and one-eyed, that everybody was clamoring to show me." Yet while it may seem this way in the aggregate, be assured that if you meet one of these ladies in the flesh. . . um. . . spirit, your boredom will vanish in a flash!

In any case, when the American travels to Europe, he is really going home, whether or not he is aware of it. While the accounts that follow may not be as detailed as those from the British Isles, don't be surprised if the experience of encountering such spirits itself will enlighten you!

Gallic Ghosts

France is a mysterious country. Her history, and, indeed, the establishment of her monarchy, is riddled with supernatural intervention. The Romans under Julius Caesar conquered the Celtic Gauls, who, like most of their race, were attached to the strange rites of the druids—human sacrifice, the use of mistletoe, the evocation of horned gods, and the like. Although the Romans were themselves no strangers to bizarre sacrifices and weird religious practices, they found the standing stones and blood-drenched sacred groves of their new province highly unsettling, to say the least. They Latinized Gaulish with a vengeance. In a few generations, save in some isolated spots, the Gauls seemed to have lost their old culture entirely.

But this is not exactly true. While it may not be, as some have said, that French is "merely Latin with a Gaulish accent," the former inhabitants have left a few traces in the modern language. For example, the words for the numbers forty, fifty, and sixty (*quarante*, *cinquante*, and *soixante*) are obviously derived from Latin and have cognates in Italian, Spanish, and the other Romance languages. But seventy and eighty, rather than being *septante* and *octante*, as one might expect, are *soixante-dix* (sixty-ten) and *quatre-vingt* (four twenties), reflecting the ancient Gaulish accounting system. So too, like the slightest of vapors, the haunting otherworldliness of the Gauls sometimes peeks out from the otherwise rigorously logical Latinity of the French mind.

Thus, when Christianity came to Gaul, it arrived on the wings of the miraculous. Sometime after A.D. 60, a boat without sails arrived in Provence, carrying a distinguished passenger list, as many chronicles and saints' lives attest. On board were the sibling saints, Lazarus (the resurrected friend of Jesus), Maximin, Martha, and Mary Magdalene; with them came the ladies' gypsy maid, Sara. Also on board were Saint Joseph of Arimathea, bearing the Holy Grail; Saint Mary of Cleophas and Saint Mary Salome; and the body of Saint Anne, mother of the Blessed Virgin. Upon reaching their new home, they scattered. Saint Joseph of Arimathea took himself and the Grail to Britain. The others went out and set up in various locales. It is perhaps typical of the French that when Saint Martha freed a town of a dragon, the grateful townsfolk renamed their municipality not after their liberatrix, but after the beast she vanquished, the *Tarasque*. So Tarascon has been called ever since.

Are all these tales true? It would be a foolhardy non-Frenchman who would deny them openly, when visiting any of the several cities which claim these saints-errant as their patrons. So it is with the story of Saint Denis the Areopagite, who, after setting up Athens as a diocese (and receiving little response) came to Paris, becoming first bishop there as well. Beheaded for his religion by the Roman authorities on a hill north of town (known ever afterwards as *Montmartre* in commemoration), he walked six miles north carrying his head to the spot where the Royal Abbey of Saint

Denis now stands. In later years, this became the necropolis of the kings of France, as Westminster Abbey is for the English monarchs.

But the Roman Empire was decaying. In 405, the legions abandoned Britain. Many of the Britons fled across the channel to escape the resulting Saxon onslaught. The place where they found refuge was the remote peninsula of Armorica, known afterwards as Little Britain or Brittany. This is why we call the island of their origin Great Britain. Brittany is now the only place in France where a Celtic language—albeit, a non-Gaulish one—is spoken in France. Like their Welsh and Cornish cousins, the Bretons live in a universe filled with strange beings. Ghosts and fairies haunt the old standing stones, and Death himself, the *Ankou*, rides about in a dark coach, picking up the souls of the departed. The Bretons also tell tales of King Arthur, the last great defender of their lost homeland, and his men. To this day, they will tell you that the magic-drenched forest of Broceliande, or Paimpont as it has come to be called, shelters not only elves and a wonder-bestowing fountain, but an imprisoned Merlin himself.

The rest of Gaul, however, came under the rule of a Germanic tribe called the Franks. Claiming descent from refugee Trojans, the barbarians were headed by a warrior named Clovis. Married to the Christian saint, Clotilde, he offered to convert to her religion if her God would grant him victory in battle. Once this victory was achieved, he kept his part of the bargain. On Christmas Day, 498, Clovis and his men received a Mass baptism at the hands of Saint Remigius, Clotilde's chaplain and bishop of the place.

At the holy man's prayer, a vial of oil descended from Heaven, born by the Holy Spirit in the form of a dove. Remigius used this oil to anoint Clovis when he crowned him King of the Franks. By virtue of this special anointing, Clovis's successors on the throne acted as miraculous healers of scrofula, banishing it by their touch. Rheims, the town where these miraculous events occurred, became as a result the preferred coronation site for the kings of France, and the dove in later centuries became the symbol of the Order of the Holy Spirit, France's answer to England's Order of the Garter.

But after a while, Clovis's descendants, the Merovingians, proved themselves to be inept rulers (despite claims of divine ancestry by the authors of such works as *Holy Blood, Holy Grail* and *The Da Vinci Code*). In time, they abdicated all responsibility for war and peace to their majordomos.

Another family, the Carolingians—the greatest of whom, Charlemagne, saved Rome from the Lombards and was duly crowned Holy Roman Emperor by Pope Saint Leo III on Christmas Day 800—displaced the Merovingians after having served as their majordomos. Charlemagne in his turn was the subject of all sorts of wondrous tales. He saw the field of stars (*Compostela*) leading to the tomb of Saint James (*Santiago*) in Spain. He discovered the tomb of Saint Mary Magdalene in Provence. Around him and his twelve paladins gathered the sort of legends that made King Arthur and his knights famous. As with Arthur, Charlemagne's death was mysterious. Although his shrine and relics may be seen in Aachen, it is said that he and his men are asleep in the German mountain, the Kaiserberg. Again, like Arthur, it is claimed that he will rise in defense of his people when needed.

But Charlemagne's version of Camelot did not survive him long, and from its ruins, feudalism was born. All across France, noble families built castles for themselves. While all claimed loyalty to the French king, they made war upon him and each other with great abandon. This stouthearted if chaotic aristocracy—with its marital scandals, interminable feuds, and constant disregard for the rights of both their serfs and their enemies—gave rise to many of the ghosts said to be haunting the surviving castles of France.

At last, one of these noblemen, the Duke of Normandy, conquered England in 1066, becoming a sovereign in his own right. But if William the Conqueror and his descendants were kings in London, they remained feudal vassals of the French king as far as

Normandy was concerned. This fact, and the convoluted mysteries of genealogy, led several English monarchs to claim the French throne, and set in motion the bloody Hundred Years' War. By 1425, northern France, including Paris and Rheims, were firmly in English hands. In his refuge at Poitiers, it did not look as though the rightful heir to the throne, the Dauphin (son of Charles VI) would ever be crowned, or that France would ever be rid of her unwelcome guests.

But in that very year, a heroine arose. Although Saint Joan of Arc was initially a friend of the local fairies in her hometown of Domremy in Lorraine, she was guided by the voices of saints on her way to victory. Even though captured and murdered via a rigged trial by the English, she began their expulsion from France. The country's independence was secured, and the French were duly convinced of God's interest in their nation.

But more—and far worse—struggles were waiting for the French. The tragedy of the Huguenot Wars was somewhat effaced by the grandeur of Louis XIV, the "Sun King," with his palaces, most notably Versailles. All that would come to an end with the tragic deaths of Louis XVI and his Austrian queen, Marie Antoinette, in the French Revolution. Indeed, no succeeding French government has rested too easily since then on a throne so vilely emptied. The bloodstained guillotine remains one of the eeriest political symbols the world has ever seen.

It should not be too surprising that with such a background, the folklore of France comprises an enormous amount of the outré. Even today, *fées* (fairies) and *lutins* (elves) represent the fairy world, the *feu-follet* (will o' the wisp) lures the unwary off swampland paths, and the fearsome *loup-garou* (werewolf) stalks its prey. Needless to say, ruined and intact castles alike boast their ghostly tenants. All of these kinds of tales traveled with French settlers overseas to Louisiana, Quebec, the West Indies, and elsewhere. The author himself literally heard such stories at his father's knee.

Indeed, throughout the French-speaking world, from Senegal to New Orleans, from Haiti to Quebec, the relationship between the living and the dead was, and to a large degree, still is, taken very seriously. After lunch on All Saints' Day, or *Toussaint*, folks go to their family plots in local cemeteries dressed in their Sunday clothes. They clean tombs and graves, weed the plots, and (in France, at any rate) arrange chrysanthemums. At nightfall they light candles. Cemeteries throughout Francophonie are ablaze with light. The following day is All Souls' Day, or *le Jour des Morts*, when, as elsewhere, special Masses for the dead are offered. It is thought in some out-of-the-way places that the dead come back to share the family meal on one or the other of those days.

In any case, the haunted châteaus we are now going to look at come by their phantasms honestly, given their histories. The uncanny is as much a part of French soil as the grape and the truffle. Now it is time to sample some of the country's supernatural wares.

Where Marie Antoinette
Holds Court—Still!

The kings of France, despite the French Revolution, have left their mark upon the realm they once ruled. From the Palais de Justice and the Louvre in downtown Paris, to the glittering châteaus of Amboise and Chambord on the Loire, to Fontainebleau and Compiegne on either end of the Île-de-France, these royal residences continue to attract awestruck visitors from around the globe. But without a doubt, the most spectacular is Versailles, located in the southwestern Parisian suburb of the same name. Here, history has been truly reenacted, at least once.

The origins of the great palace we see today were very humble. In 1623, Louis XIII (Louis XIV's father) built a small brick hunting lodge at Versailles. So popular did it become with both Louises—fond, as most monarchs are, of hunting—that they made some enormous additions. But Versailles would soon have a more important role.

Louis XIV, before he came of age, lived through attempts—first by the Parlement of Paris (a court, not a legislature) in 1648, and then by the high nobility of France, starting in 1650—to take control of the country. These two events were called the *Fronde*. They traumatized the young king. He resolved that neither nobility nor bureaucracy would ever challenge the supremacy of the monarchy again. His campaign in this area was partly fought in the realm of centralizing administration and fighting foreign wars of expansion (all of which ended in defeat and were ruinously expensive). But a large part of the royal offensive was to be cultural, including patronage of the arts and education, assistance to religion, and the like. But most obvious was the king's creation of palatial architecture. Versailles would be the cornerstone of this effort.

While the king's ornamental lifestyle accomplished its task, it also wore him down. Realizing this problem, Louis designed and established a nearby refuge for himself called the Trianon, where he could withdraw from the rigors of court life. But these bucolic pleasures and the business of court and family life could not remove the sad realities of life. Support for the American Revolution bankrupted the country. Intrigues against the hapless king on the part of some of the well-placed (including his cousin, the duke of Orleans), combined with economic woes gave rise to the French Revolution.

On October 5, 1789, a mob of ruffians attacked Versailles, and brought the royal family back to Paris. There they dwelt, increasingly as prisoners, in the palace of the Tuileries. On August 10, 1792, another mob attacked their palace. Most of the king's Swiss Guard were killed defending them, and the royal family was imprisoned outright. The king, after a mock trial, was murdered by guillotine on January 21, 1793, and his queen was similarly dealt with later that year. Two years later, their young son, the "Lost Dauphin," died of abuse and neglect in prison.

Of course, many thousands of others died at the hands of the revolutionaries, in France and throughout Europe. The period between 1789 and 1815 was the bloodiest Europe had ever seen up until that time—or would see again, until the "enlightened" days of the twentieth century, when wars in the name of "freedom" would dwarf the excesses of the Revolutionary era.

In a sense, every historical event lives on, both in its consequences and in the lives of the descendants of those who survive it. In the first year of the twentieth century, however, it appeared that something more tangible might linger at Versailles. Prior to this time, there had already been whispered accounts of a "gray lady," whom locals identified as Marie Antoinette, and who might be seen from time to time on the grounds of the Trianon.

On August 10, 1901, Anne Moberly and Eleanor Jourdain, principal and vice principal of St. Hugh's College, Oxford, decided to add Versailles to their French vacation. Having toured the palace and enjoyed the refreshments then sold in the Hall of Mirrors, they set off to explore the gardens. They were particularly keen on seeing the Petit Trianon.

The gardens of Versailles are extensive, and the Petit Trianon is almost a mile from the palace. Even though equipped with a map, the ladies were gossiping about friends at home, and paid little attention to where they were walking. After they had wandered about for a while, they passed a deserted farmhouse, noticing an old plow lying by the side of the road. When they looked at their map, they realized they were lost. Finally, they came to a group of buildings. Fortunately, there were two men dressed in long gray-green coats and tricornes standing nearby, one holding a shovel. From their appearance, and a nearby wheelbarrow, the ladies concluded that they were gardeners. When asked for directions, the pair directed the women to walk straight on.

This they did. But as the ladies walked, both became increasingly depressed, despite the bright summer weather. They made another wrong turn, and happened upon a sort of gazebo. Seated upon the rail was a man with a "rough, dark complexion" and a "repulsive face." Miss Jourdain immediately had a feeling that he was "evil." Becoming fearful, she ignored him, as did Miss Moberly.

While they walked on, a man ran up behind them, shouting breathlessly, "Mesdames, mesdames." Tall, and dressed in a sombrero-like hat and heavy black cloak, his handsome face bright red with exertion, he spoke rapidly in French and gestured to the women. By his signals, they thought that he intended for them to turn right and cross a bridge. Miss Moberly thought he had said something about "looking for the house."

Doing as they were bade, the pair soon found themselves at the back of the Petit Trianon. Miss Moberly saw a woman seated on a chair under the balustrade of the rear terrace, sketching or reading. In Miss Moberly's own words: "She had on a shady white hat, perched on a good deal of fair hair that fluffed around her forehead. Her light summer dress was arranged on her shoulders in handkerchief fashion, and there was a little line of either green or gold near the edge of the handkerchief. . . Her dress was long-waisted, with a good deal of fullness in the skirt. . . . I thought she was a tourist, but that her dress was old-fashioned and rather unusual."

The educators continued on, toward the stairs that led to the rear terrace. The seated woman turned and looked at Miss Moberly, who saw that the woman was not young, and that "there was something unattractive about her appearance." The ladies continued to walk around the building, when a door opened and a footman came out and slammed the door behind him. They asked him where the entrance was. He directed them, and they found it at last, coming into the midst of a wedding party. The teachers toured the Petit Trianon without further incident.

Finished with Versailles, they took tea at a nearby hotel and returned to Paris. Apparently, at the time, neither thought that there was anything odd about their experience. They did not bother discussing the visit for about a week. Eventually, Miss Moberly asked her friend, "Do you think that the grounds of the Petit Trianon are haunted?"

"Yes, I do," replied Miss Jourdain.

They talked about it a bit more, but the matter was dropped for the moment. Three months later, Miss Jourdain visited Miss Moberly at her Oxford home. Mentioning the woman sitting at the back of the Petit Trianon, Miss Moberly was surprised when her friend declared that she had not seen her. Since it was apparent to them that each might have seen something different, the ladies agreed to write separate accounts of what they had each experienced. They made a pact to research the historical aspects of the occurrence further. Their detective work turned up some interesting facts.

Miss Jourdain inquired of friends whether they had heard stories about ghosts at the Petit Trianon. In response, a French friend said that Marie Antoinette could be seen sitting outside the Petit Trianon, wearing a light hat and a pink dress, on August 10, the date that the royal family was imprisoned after the slaughter of their guards at the Tuileries. Misses Moberly and Jourdain had visited on August 10, 109 years after this historical event. Moreover, this helpful source added, the whole complex was haunted by Marie Antoinette's friends, acquaintances, and servants. This convinced Miss Jourdain that her friend had seen the ghost of the doomed queen, and that they had both seen the ghosts of her companions. The ladies decided that what they had seen had not been the present Petit Trianon, but rather the same building as it was over a century before.

As it happened, school duties saw Miss Jourdain taking numerous trips to Paris and Versailles with her students between 1902 and 1904. She took advantage of these opportunities to try and re-create their walk, but the gazebo and the bridge were missing. In July 1904, Miss Jourdain and Miss Moberly visited Versailles together, but were still unable to find the gazebo or the bridge.

They concluded that they must have gone back in time to a date when both objects were present. Furthermore, during this later visit, there were tourists everywhere, whereas on their earlier visit they had only seen the two gardeners, the ugly man at the gazebo, the running man, and the seated lady.

Still seeking proof that they had time-traveled, they consulted longtime workers at Versailles, as well as various libraries and bookstores. Their research was revealing. Although none of the current employees wore the uniforms the ladies had seen on the presumed gardeners that day, back in the eighteenth century, the queen's guards had indeed worn such clothing. And while the gazebo was nowhere to be found, such a structure did appear on an old map they discovered, but it had been demolished well before 1901.

The ugly man answered the description of the Comte de Vaudreuil, an enemy of Marie Antoinette. Their out-of-breath acquaintance, the running man, wore the uniform of an eighteenth-century royal messenger, while the woman Miss Moberly saw, sitting by the terrace of the Petit Trianon, resembled a painting of Marie Antoinette by artist Wertmüller, even down to the clothes she wore.

They had seen a plow on their first visit, and they subsequently learned that while no plows were kept in the gardens of Versailles in 1901, such tools had been displayed on the grounds in 1789. Although they could not find the bridge they had crossed, they did discover that a bridge had existed there in 1789. Moreover, when they revisited the spot where the footman had rushed out to direct them, they found the door barred and bolted shut, as it had been for many years.

Since neither of them had been familiar with these historical details when they first visited in 1901, they concluded that they must have entered some sort of time warp that day. The women were convinced that Marie Antoinette had doubtless thought long and hard about the last day she spent at Versailles in 1789—August

10—the very date of their first visit. Even though Marie Antoinette had not been at Versailles on August 10, 1792, she must have *thought* about returning there. In their minds, it stood to reason that they had somehow been transported back in time by the sheer power of the dead queen's emotions and memories.

In 1911, the ladies published their story and subsequent research (including their time-warp thesis) under the pseudonyms of Miss Morison and Miss Lamont, in a book entitled *An Adventure*. It sold eleven thousand copies by 1913. Despite the book's popularity, critics argued that the two women had either gotten lost, or had been mistaken in what they thought they saw that day.

Eleanor Sidgwick of the Society for Psychical Research in London wrote that their story lacked credibility because they had been talking to each other, paying little attention to their surroundings, and therefore, might have easily been mistaken about what actually happened. Furthermore, Mrs. Sidgwick opined, since they wrote their accounts three months after the fact, their memories might have been faulty. She was not surprised that they could not retrace their path, since they were probably unable to recall exactly where they had been.

Miss Jourdain died in 1924, and Miss Moberly in 1937. After their deaths their identities were revealed as authors of the book. Because of the respectable reputations they had earned in academia, this spurred a more intense look into their claims. In 1950, W. H. Salter—who had carefully read Misses Jourdain's and Moberly's correspondence with the Society for Psychical Research—decided that many of the details included in the accounts they claimed to have written in 1901 actually dated from 1906, when the ladies had concluded their research. Thus, to a skeptic, their claims of being unable to have known about the layout of Versailles in 1789 were exploded.

We will probably never know, from this side of the grave, what the ladies actually saw that day in 1901—unless, of course, someone repeats their experience. But they certainly must have seen something. Having been lost with his late father near the Trianon in 1991, this author can vouch for the mysterious spell of the area. While one might not want to spend time with the Comte de Vaudreuil, the gentle, artistic shade of Marie Antoinette might not be a bad companion. In any case, the history, glory, tragedy, and joy of Versailles await you—and perhaps, something more!

Château de Versailles
RP 834 - 78008 Versailles Cedex
France

Tel: +33 (0) 1 30 83 75 48
Fax: +33 (0) 1 30 83 75 19
http://www.chateauversailles.fr/en/
E-mail: service.multimedia@chateauversailles.fr

The Lady in Green Walks

Visitors to Brissac, in Anjou, are always struck by the fairy-tale appearance of the town's château. One could well imagine *Sleeping Beauty* or some other such story being set here. It is a magical place, still in the hands of one family after many centuries, and renowned for its haunting by *la Dame Verte*, or the "Green Lady." But Château Brissac is typical of many such places in the Province of Anjou.

Located on the Loire, Anjou is a province rich in history—of course, that usually means a long chronicle of warfare and crime, as well as religious faith and grandeur. In very early days, as Christianity spread through the province, monks opened monasteries in St. Florent-le-Vieil, St. Aubin d'Angers, and St. Maur de Glanfeuil. Proper management of these houses led to great wealth. Unfortunately, this in turn helped attract the attentions of the Vikings to Anjou in the ninth century. These unwelcome visitors sailed up the Loire, burning and sacking not just abbeys, but market towns and castles as well. When Brittany was attacked, the Bretons came to Anjou's aid, led by their doughty count, Robert the Strong. Alas, he fell at Brissarthe in 866 while fighting the Norse. Anjou eventually became a possession of the dukes of Normandy, and so, of the kings of England. Once restored to French rule, the province was given to a branch of the French royal family, who set up as kings of their own in Naples—the House of Anjou. But while sovereign in Italy, they remained vassals at home.

Then, in the fifteenth century, René of Anjou went on to alter castles into châteaus. Over sixty of these castles and great houses survive in Anjou today, many owned by the descendants of their builders. But of all these buildings, one of the best known is the Château de Brissac in the Commune of Brissac-Quincé, in the department of Maine-et-Loire.

The first count of Anjou originally built the château in the eleventh century. After King Philip II of France defeated the English, he gave the property to one Guillaume des Roches. But in the fifteenth century, Pierre de Brézé, the chief minister to King Charles VII, rebuilt the castle. His son, Jacques, grand seneschal of Normandy, and bearing the title of Count de Maulévrier, married Charlotte of France. She in turn was the illegitimate daughter of Charles VII and Agnes Sorel, former employee of King René. Despite her irregular birth, she was the beloved half sister of King Louis XI, Charles's son.

Unhappily, this marriage would not end well. Jacques discovered his wife at the manor of Rouvres, close to Poitiers, in the arms of one of her huntsmen. Accounts differ as to how events proceeded. Some maintain that Jacques administered over a hundred blows of his sword to the couple, while others maintain that he strangled her in the Chapel Tower at Brissac. Whatever the case, neither Charlotte nor her boyfriend survived the encounter. Louis XI was outraged when he learned the news, immediately vowing revenge. He had the grand seneschal arrested and flung into prison for a few years. He then prevailed upon a court to sentence Jacques to death, and to confiscate all of his property.

This was not entirely carried out, however. De Brézé saved his head by giving the king all his properties. Louis XI in turn gave these to his nephew and godson, Louis de Brézé, Jacques's own son. Three years after his accession, Louis's successor, Charles VIII, quashed the judgment and returned to Jacques de Brézé his titles and lands.

In time, the castle came to the Cossé family, who were created dukes de Brissac, and went on to occupy a distinguished place at court. In republican France, the current duke of Brissac and his family, although no longer playing a governmental role, are social lions—they are pillars of the aristocratic Jockey Club de Paris, and the duke is master of the Fontainebleau Hunt. But they also retain the château whose name gave the family its title. Brissac is open for tours. Annually, the château's gilded theater plays host to the annual Val de Loire festival.

Although Brissac and its current owners are firmly rooted in the present, they cannot escape the past—anymore than anyone else can. One tenant has survived the changes in ownership and the destruction wrought by Huguenots and Jacobins. She is an apparition called *la Dame Verte* (or the Green Lady), who walks in the tower of the chapel. Wearing the green dress that she is named for, and with the face of a corpse, this ghastly revenant is believed to be the murdered Charlotte de France. Whether sliced, diced, or strangled, she has apparently never gotten over the death she suffered at the hands of her wronged husband. While the duke and his family take her in stride, many a visitor has been shocked by her appearance. If you take the fascinating tour of this exciting château, say a quick prayer for Charlotte in the chapel—should you encounter her, you won't regret it!

Château de Brissac
49320 Brissac
France

Tel: +33 (0) 2 41 91 22 21
Fax: +33 (0) 2 41 91 25 60
http://www.chateau-brissac.fr/
E-mail: chateau-brissac@wanadoo.fr

A Literate Ghost

Mention "Burgundy" to most Americans, and they will immediately think of red wine. Certainly, grapes are one of the greatest assets the province possesses, but there are others. Burgundy gave rise to two of the greatest monastic orders in the Church—the Cluniacs and the Cistercians. It was at Paray-le-Monial, in Burgundy, that Saint Margaret Mary Alacoque had her famous visions of the Sacred Heart of Jesus, an image now known all over the world. At Paray as well, in the nineteenth century, the Hieron was founded. As a papally approved institute, dedicated to the study of both Catholicism and the Kabbalah, the Hieron has figured prominently in the *Holy Blood, Holy Grail* mythology as a sort of prototype for the "Priory of Scion." Given this background, it makes sense that the ghost we will look at here was renowned in life for her wit and fine writing.

Constant wars and conflicts throughout the centuries left their mark. Burgundy's noble families reinforced their castles, lived their lives, and inevitably, spawned ghosts.

Located in the north of Burgundy, one and a half hours from Paris, La Puisaye is filled with deep woods and ruined castles. The people were considered secretive by outsiders, and known for their strange tales of the werewolves, fairies, and witches that haunted their forests. Not surprisingly, the environment has given birth to a few of France's wilder writers, most notably Collette, who was raised in the town of St. Sauveur-de-Puisaye.

But it is the town of St. Fargeau, dominated by its castle, which is considered the capital of La Puisaye. The Château de St. Fargeau owes its origins to the fifth century, when either the Romans or the Burgundians built a stronghold on the site to secure the place during the chaos of that period. In the year 980, Bishop Éribert of Auxerre turned the castle into a hunting lodge. From the tenth to the fifteenth centuries, a succession of noteworthy owners took over the place in turn. At last, in 1453, Antoine de Chabannes molded the castle into its current configuration, a hexagon with six great towers.

Louis XIV's cousin, Marie Louise d'Orleans (the "Great Mademoiselle"), altered the château's appearance considerably. Marie-Louise was not too happy to arrive at the château. Although she was a relative of the king—like their mutual kinsman, the "Great Condé," governor of Burgundy—she had worked against him during the Fronde. But Louis was merciful: Instead of execution, in 1652 she was given five years of exile. She chose St. Fargeau for her luxurious house arrest because it was only three days from Paris by coach, and gossip from the court could still reach her there.

To further cushion her stay, she appointed Louis Le Vau, the architect responsible for the redesign of the Louvre, to a similar task at St. Fargeau: the alteration of a medieval castle, whose major goal had been military defense, into a comfortable château. Amongst other alterations, Le Vau heightened the towers and enlarged the windows—a measure unthinkable during the bad old days of constant warfare.

"La Grande Mademoiselle" did not waste her time during her confinement, but instead used it to write. In 1653 she published a satirical account of life at court. Then she commenced her *Memoires*, and began the seventeen literary portraits she contributed to the salon collection entitled *Divers Portraits*.

Louis allowed her to return to court in 1657, where she continued her writing career, branching out into satirical fiction. But while she kept her sense of humor, her heart led her astray. Refusing to marry the king of Portugal at her cousin's order, she was again exiled to St. Fargeau for a year in 1663. Allowed back to Paris, Marie Louise promptly lost her heart to the young Comte de Lauzun, one of Louis's guard officers. In 1670, she decided to marry him. Her cousin first approved of the match, then changed his mind and sent her lover to prison. She worked tirelessly for his release over the following decade. He was freed at last in 1681, and they married.

Alas, what one thinks is one's heart's desire often turns out not to be the best thing for it. Lauzun may have been handsome, but he apparently had defects in the character department. His interest in his wife turned out to be primarily financial. After running through her vast fortune in a few years, they were separated in 1684. An older but wiser Marie Louise, although impoverished, devoted the rest of her life to pious works and reflection. She wrote two more books, one on suffering, and the other on the vanity of the code of "honor."

Château St. Fargeau was purchased by the Lepeletier family in 1713. Shortly after, the head of the family came to be called the Marquis de Lepeletier-Saint Fargeau. Louis Michel, owner of the château at the outbreak of the revolution, abandoned his title and joined the Jacobins. When the question of killing Louis XVI came up for a vote before the Assembly, Citizen Lepeletier voted for death. Although that action won him kudos from the other Jacobins, it would eventually cost him his life. Shortly after the deed, Lepeletier was dining in a fashionable restaurant in the Palais Royale. A former bodyguard of the king knifed him at the table. The government considered Lepeletier a hero; he was buried with state honors at the Pantheon, and the famed artist David was commissioned to paint his portrait.

But with the return of saner times, the regicide's body was removed from its esteemed resting place, and the portrait conveyed to the château and hidden there by his daughter—its whereabouts remain one of St. Fargeau's two major mysteries. In time, the château fell into disrepair, only to be rescued in 1979 when professional restorers Michel and Jacques Guyot bought the property. It took them two decades to restore it, and the result is a gem that attracts tourists from all over to this remote corner of France.

Nevertheless, all of this restoration has not dislodged the château's permanent resident, la Grande Mademoiselle. Employees and visitors alike have encountered her shade, recognizing her immediately from her portrait. She is most often seen in the cellars, looking deep in thought. Why there? Possibly because this is the least altered portion of her former domain. She does not frighten those who encounter her, so it could be that she continues her quiet meditations on the vanity of worldly things—with the insight that only death can provide. If you encounter her, perhaps she will share her wisdom with you.

M. Michel Guyot
Château St. Fargeau
89170 St. Fargeau
France

Tel: +33 (0) 3 86 74 05 67
http://www.chateau-de-saint-fargeau.com/

Her Broken Heart Won't Heal

The province of Aquitaine straddled the border of French and English territory during much of the Hundred Years' War. As might be expected, this bequeathed to the region a history of bloody conflict, and so, consequently, many castles. But the south of France in general is very different from the north. Colonized first by the Romans, it was always more Latinate; in many areas, the locals speak Occitan, a language closer to Catalan than French.

Since the days of the Cathars in the thirteenth century, odd cults have flourished from time to time in the region. Legends abound there—not just of ghosts and witches, but of the devil himself, apparently evoked by the Cathars, according to local stories. In a more conventional mode, various pilgrimage routes have crisscrossed the region, as folk from the rest of Europe traveled to the Spanish shrine of Santiago de Compostela, and Iberians made their way to Rome and Canterbury. One of the most important stops on these two trails was and is the fortress town of Rocamadour.

Founded by Roland—the heroic but ill-starred nephew of Charlemagne, who would later fall at the pass of Roncesvalles—the town site was selected by its founder, who plunged his sword, Durandal, into the earth. Rocamadour boasted a shrine to the Virgin even before the tenth century. But in 1166, the body of Saint Amadour was found, and the town became a pilgrimage center in its own right. Despite the devastation wrought in the area by the Huguenot Wars, by the seventeenth century the liturgical pieces plundered by the Huguenots were replaced. Two centuries later, pilgrimages to Rocamadour were revived.

On the road from Rocamadour to Santiago was a spot also much used by pilgrims to Rome called the *Roumieux*. From this name came the title of Roumegouse, and a tower was built on the site to protect travelers. In the tenth century, the Barons of Gramat owned the place; later it was given to the Church of Cahors for use as a leprosarium. In time, Roumegouse passed to the Lord of Castelnau. Evolving from a mere backwater, the château became an important stronghold for Hugues II de Castelnau, one of the most renowned noblemen of Aquitaine.

But the château has also seen its share of romantic episodes. Hugues's kinswoman, the Lady Resplendine de Rignac, was engaged to a knight who set off on the First Crusade. Although that episode was successful, and Jerusalem duly liberated from the Turks, Resplendine's fiancé fell during the siege of the Holy City. Upon hearing the news, she died of a broken heart.

During these centuries, the region was in a bad way. War, robbery, and murder were common, as the French struggled to repel Arabs and English at various times, and even each other. As a result, Roumegouse was often destroyed and rebuilt. At last, when peace was established during the seventeenth century, the château—no longer boasting a resident family—fell into ruin.

But revival was on the way, in the form of the Cavalie family. Having purchased the crumbling castle at the beginning of the nineteenth century, the owners built the hamlet Roumegouse around the front entrance of the château. Reconstruction of the castle began in 1893, under the direction of Jean Pisie, husband to Victorine Cavalie. The task was completed in two years. Monsieur Pisie died at the beginning of World War II in 1940.

Used as a hospital by the Resistance during the war, afterwards it was bought by General de Gaulle's hairdresser. The Laine family purchased the place in 1965, opening it the following year and hosting famous guests from then until now. Second-generation owners Luce and Jean-Louis Laine now operate the hotel, offering Louis XIV and Second Empire–style guestrooms, and dining rooms that serve local cuisine.

But the elegant and enjoyable amenities cannot conceal one guest who will not leave. Resplendine de Rignac haunts the corridors of the château, and while her apparition has frightened both staff and visitors, she has perfected another trick since the château became a hotel. Not content with mere visibility, Resplendine will enter guests' rooms in the middle of the night and wake them by pinching them. Although she does not appear when she does this, her actions have their effect. Many to whom she has so ministered check out immediately, regardless of the hour. But should you find yourself in that position, don't be too hasty. By all accounts, the joys of the château warrant lengthy exposure—which may be why Resplendine has never left.

Château de Roumegouse
Rignac 46 500
France

Tel: (800) 359-4827
http://www.chateauderoumegouse.com/Factsandfigures.htm

A Dungeon Makes a Ghost

Perigord is another region of southern France, famous not only for its strange folklore of witchcraft and second sight, but also for its wines, and above all, black truffles. Despite these pleasures, Perigord too has suffered centuries of relentless warfare, and has its own inheritance of castles. Its spiritual state at the time of the revolution may be gauged by the fact that the corrupt Talleyrand was its bishop (although events allowed him to jettison his miter and eventually serve as Napoleon's foreign minister).

Founded in the eighth century, Perigord's capital, Sarlat, was yet another border town between the French and English. Passed back and forth at the price of great bloodshed, Sarlat definitively passed to France in 1370. Henry IV made it a diocese with a cathedral, but for the most part, the town remained quiet until the railroad arrived in the nineteenth century.

Just outside Sarlat is the Château de Puymartin. Erected in 1269, both the château and its village of the same name were border installations, like Sarlat. Warfare took its toll, however. The château was looted and stripped of its ramparts, towers, and roofing. But in 1450, Radulphe de Saint Clar rebuilt and enlarged the ruin. In the ensuing centuries, the Saint Clar family (eventually ennobled as the counts de Montbron) added a spiral staircase, a room of honor decorated with Aubusson tapestries, French-style beams, and incredible furniture to the château's inventory.

Unfortunately, tragedies were also added, as is the case with any family that stays long enough in one location. In the sixteenth century, Therese de Saint Clar, who had taken advantage of her husband's absence during the Huguenot Wars by finding herself a lover, received a surprise visit from her spouse. As lord of the domain, he had the right to punish malefactors, and had his wife imprisoned for fifteen years in a small room in the North Tower. There she languished, deprived of visitors, books, or conversation. When she died, her corpse was sealed in the same room. Eventually, she was properly buried, and the room in which she had endured so much is now open for visitors.

In the next century, the family put the affair and the grim little chamber connected with it to rest by creating the "mythological room." An historical landmark, it boasts outstanding *grisailles* (paintings in black and white on egg white) depicting Greek mythological scenes.

This sort of resilience stood the counts de Montbron in good stead, for they have survived revolutions and regime changes in good order, all the while managing to hold on to Puymartin. It is in fact the present count and countess who will host you at Puymartin. This tenacity is not restricted to living members of the family, for Therese de Saint Clar remains in her old home. Nicknamed the *Dame Blanche* (or White Lady) for the dress she wears, family, staff, and guests often see her wending her way through the hallways to the little room in the North Tower where she ended her days. Even the current count has seen her on this trip of hers, and so is sympathetic to those of his guests who share the "privilege"!

Comtesse de Montbron
Château de Puymartin
24200 Sarlat
France

Tel: +33 (0) 5 53 59 29 97
Fax: +33 (0) 5 53 29 87 52
E-mail: bestofperigord@perigord.com

Spirits in the Land of Dante

taly was the birthplace of the Roman Empire and the Renaissance, and is the headquarters of the Catholic Church. Its many
cities are filled with extraordinary art, and it is second only to
France in the quality of its food and wine (if indeed it is second!).
Artists like Michelangelo, Rafael, and Leonardo; writers like Dante,
Boccacio, and Petrarch; composers like Verdi and Cherubini—all
speak of the cultural genius of the Italians. Rome conquered the
known world, and Saint Peter's setting up the papacy there ensured
the Eternal City a spiritual supremacy over hundreds of millions of
souls that endures to this day.

Nevertheless, for all their brilliance, the Italians have had a
dark history. The fall of the empire ushered in the barbarian invasions, which eventually led to the fragmentation of the peninsula
into hundreds of city-states. Although these coalesced over time
into larger regions, it was not until 1870 that the country was
united. The fissures caused by this disunity remain part of the
social and political fabric of the country. Although they were

united by language and religion, the hatred that these conflicts sowed between Italians was phenomenal. Noble families, when they could not dominate the towns, held themselves aloof in their castles playing one city against the other, and the Pope against the emperor. With this atmosphere, Machiavelli fit right in. Even when unity was finally achieved, the weak state of the country brought about the rise of strongman Mussolini.

A similar paradox holds true in the world of the unseen. Since the time of Saint Peter, the country has literally crawled with saints and miracles. The liquefying blood of Saint Januarius in Naples, the oil of Saint Nicholas oozing still from his bones at Bari, the Holy House of the Blessed Virgin at Loreto, and the bread and wine turned to actual flesh and blood at Mass in Lanciano are just a few of the many items awaiting the searcher for the miraculous in Italy. There are so many shrines in the country that a lifetime of travel would not allow the pilgrim a chance to pray at a tenth of them. Rome's Purgatory Museum at the Church of Sacro Cuore del Suffragio, with its macabre collection of various artifacts bearing burn marks from being touched by "returnees" (who ask for a certain number of prayers or Masses to spring them from purgatory), is a testimony to the "bright side" of the spirit world.

But there is another side to the spiritual in Italy. There are many stories of devil worship. At the turn of the nineteenth century, when renovations were being done at Rome's Palazzo Borghese, a satanic chapel, fitted up for a Black Mass, was found behind a sealed-up door. In remoter districts, the *Strega*, or witch, may hold entire villages in her fearsome thrall. Since Italian folklore is filled with tales of ghosts and hauntings, there are few areas without ruins that are reputed to be haunted.

It is this strange duality to which we now turn our attention. Details are few, and the traveler will have to win the confidence of the locals if he wants to learn more. But patience will be rewarded. In Italy, everything seems larger than life, and this is as true of hauntings as anything else.

171

Deaths in the Family

The town of Soragna in the province of Parma boasts two castles. One belonged to the Pallavicini clan, the other, the "Rocca," to the Lupi. The Lupis have lived at the Rocca since the end of the eleventh century. In 1347, Emperor Charles IV named their lands an imperial fief, giving them some stature among their neighbors. This was needed, as even in their block-like fortress, they were small fish in a big and dangerous pond. Such nearby families as the Visconti more than once attempted to eject them from their small domain.

But heredity bestowed problems beyond even the wily Lupi's ability to control. Diofebo Lupi died in 1514 without any direct heirs. He did, however, make his maternal nephew, Giampaolo Meli, his legal successor. Various greedy relatives keen on making Soragna their own disputed Diofebo's will. One of these was Giuliano de Medici, who had the support of his relative, Pope Leo X. Nonetheless, on April 10, 1530, Emperor Charles V gave

Giampaolo Meli not only the Lupi property, but also the right to add the extinct family name Lupi to his own, and to have the imperial eagle added to his coat of arms.

His son, Diofebo II, married Cassandra Marinoni, who was nicknamed Donna Cenerina. While visiting her sister Lucrezia in Cremona in 1573, she was murdered by her brother-in-law, Giulio Anguissola, and his henchmen. Of course, Lucrezia was the primary victim, but Giulio could not leave a witness. Nevertheless, word got out, and the governor of Milan and King Philip II of Spain ordered his arrest and sentenced him to death. But he escaped, and Cassandra's death went unavenged. That might explain her subsequent behavior.

But this miscarriage of justice did not affect the family unduly. In 1709, Emperor Josef I promoted Giampaolo IV to the rank of Sovereign Prince of the Holy Roman Empire. Soragna thus became an independent state, with the right to mint coin, much to the annoyance of its neighbors, the Farnese of Parma and the Spanish in Milan. In keeping with his new status, Prince Giampolo completely redecorated the castle in lavish baroque fashion, and installed a throne room. This state of affairs lasted until 1805, when Napoleon annexed the region to France, and put control of the town under the new city government of Soragna. Although French control is long gone, the Meli Lupi family remain purely landholders. Even so, the family has continued with little annoyance to occupy their castle in peace, down to the current holder, Prince Diofebo VI.

But the prince is not the only family member in residence. Cassandra does come back from time to time. In particular, she makes herself known when a member of the family is about to die. Gian Franco, majordomo to the current prince, has witnessed Cassandra's manifestations twice. Back in 1963, an uncle of the then prince was ill at a neighboring house. The family was getting into the car when all the doors and windows on the ground floor, inside and out, started banging open and shut by themselves. Hearing this, the prince said sadly, "At this point, there's no more need for us to go." Sure enough, a little while later the news came that his uncle was dead.

Two decades later, Gian Franco was trying to sleep on a hot August night. Unable to do so, he began to hear the rapid opening and shutting of doors and windows somewhere in the house. He figured out that the sounds were coming from the direction of the drawing room, Cassandra's favorite room in life. Then, chamber by chamber, more and more of the apertures started banging away. Soon, the sounds of heavy furniture moving back and forth were added. The old butler was paralyzed with fright. Then, all of a sudden, the noises stopped dead.

Since the prince and his family were away in France, Gian was the ranking individual in the house. He went down to the servants' quarters to find everyone awake and scared. They all sat down in the kitchen, and Gian passed out glasses of grappa. All of the servants knew what the event meant. Sure enough, the phone rang a little while later. In Burgundy, the prince had died.

The new prince, Diofebo VI, has encountered Cassandra as well. In January 1993, when his mother, Violetta, was ill, Diofebo sat by her bedside. He watched as the two heavy doors of her wardrobe swung open. He got up and locked them, but the same thing happened twice more, despite the doors being locked. Glancing at his watch, he saw that it was 5:00 A.M. Sure enough, the dowager princess of Soragna died at that precise time, three days later.

Cassandra's ghost has played a more benevolent role in the prince's life as well. Back in 1975, when he was serving as an army cadet, he was on maneuvers. Suddenly, a force like a great hand forced him to bend over. As he did so, a hail of machine-gun bullets passed right over him. Shortly after that, he was riding his motorcycle in the area around the castle, when the vehicle suddenly slowed. Despite his attempts to apply great pressure to the accelerator stick, the thing would not speed up. Just then, a truck pulled in front of him, which he surely would have smacked into were it not for the inexplicable slowing. The prince is convinced that it was Cassandra who saved his life both times.

So when you visit Rocca di Soragna, so long as you harbor no ill plans for the family, fear not. Even if Cassandra does act up while you are there, remember that it has nothing to do with you—it's all in the family!

Rocca di Soragna
Piazza Meli Lupi, 5
43019 Soragna (PR)
Italy

Tel: +39 0521 6 92 81
Fax: +39 0521 69 46 66

A Royal Haunting

The dukes of Savoy, like the electors of Brandenburg in Germany, were consumed with the drive for constant expansion. Native to a small section of what is now southeast France, from their little capital at Chambery they were able to take hold of Piedmont. Shifting their capital to Turin (to which they brought the famous shroud, an ancestor having acquired it during the Crusades), they began the course of expansion that would end with their ascension to the throne of Italy in 1870. Alas, their hold on that shaky throne lasted a mere seventy-six years.

All of that lay far in the future, however, when, in 1659 Duke Carlo Emanuele II built Venaria Reale (literally, "royal hunting") as a hunting lodge outside his capital. This was no mere cabin for weekend shooting. By the seventeenth century, royal hunts had become ritualistic activities, even more splendid than the fox and deer hunting on horseback so many of us know from the movies, complete with the red coats, hunting horns, baying hounds, and special daggers for dispatching of the prey.

While all of that was, indeed, part of it, there were also musicians, special meals before and afterwards, opening festivities, and the like. Hunting represented the bond between the ruler and the land, and underscored the monarch's psychological role as protector of the people from the things that dwelt there. The chase was done for spiritual reasons as much as for physical—even as the remaining monarchs of the world continue the tradition today.

Thus a great deal of time, money, and thought went into the building of this palace, for such it was. By the time the place was completed in 1675, the complex comprised a village, royal palace, and gardens extending over a mile and a half. In 1693, invading French troops plundered and wrecked Venaria Reale, forcing the duke at that time, Vittorio Amedeo II, to undertake an extensive restoration. But Vittorio had great ambitions; he wanted to be a king. He therefore resolved to remake the palace along the lines of Versailles, then the acme of royal residences—despite his enmity toward Louis XIV.

Although his alliance with the Holy Roman Emperor in successive wars with France probably had rather more to do with it than his building program (only half completed, in the end), Vittorio Amedeo realized his dream. By the time of the Treaty of Utrecht in 1713, not only had he expanded his territory around Piedmont, but he had also acquired Sicily as well. Since Sicily was a kingdom, Vittorio was now a king, a title he retained when he traded Sicily for Sardinia in 1720. But he was not done with his work. Until he abdicated in favor of his son ten years later (he would die in 1732), the new sovereign introduced all sorts of reforms into his lands. He introduced Italy's first land and property register, in order to avoid unjust taxation. He also reorganized the University of Turin, giving the Jesuits control of what we would call postgraduate classes. Vittorio also streamlined and reformed the bureaucracy. But it is probably Venaria Reale that he considers his greatest achievement. After all, that is where you may see him today.

Since his death, members of the royal family (at least until they were banished by new republican authorities fearful of a restoration in 1946), staff, and visitors have seen Sardinia's first king wandering about the palace galleries and the stables. Wrapped in a black cape, he appears wary, as though fearful of an attempt on his life—were that possible. He is accompanied by the odor of bergamot, an herb he loved in life and cultivated by hand in the royal garden. In his left hand the king holds the reins of a white horse that paws the ground, apparently anxious to be off. In the night, for illumination, Vittorio clutches what appears at first to be a long, gilded candlestick. In reality, it is a burning breadstick (*grissino*). Why would he light his way with such a curious thing? It turns out that when Vittorio was a young duke, he was suffering from an intestinal malady that looked to be fatal. A cure was despaired of, until his court doctor, Don Baldo Pecchio, began feeding him the local breadsticks as his sole diet over a six-month period. He recovered in seemingly miraculous fashion, and since then the humble sticks have been called "this noble food and medicine" by the folk who live nearby.

This bizarre apparition, given his apparent suspicion, may not be aware of current conditions. Should you see him, do not let him know that despite all his efforts for his subjects, his crown has fallen and his descendants are exiles. Who knows what would happen if you did!

Venaria Reale
Piazza della Repubblica 4
Venaria Reale (TO)
Italy

Tel: + 39 011 559 22 11
Fax: + 39 011 432 27 91
http://www.lavenaria.it/ita/index.htm
http://www.reggiavenariareale.it/
E-mail: info.venariar@reteunitaria.piemonte.it
E-mail: posta@reggiavenariareale.it

Shadows of the Past

Like Italy, Germany has a strange duality to its nature. On the one hand, few peoples can equal the riches of German literature, music, and philosophy. Across the truncated German countryside, three indisputably German provinces—East Prussia, Pomerania, and Silesia—were lost in 1945. Considering what they had annexed and lost in the years prior, of course, to many this was a fair exchange. But descendants of those expelled from those regions can be forgiven if they do not see it that way. Countless gems of Romanesque, Gothic, and Baroque architecture abound in every village. One can only suppose how much more there was before the bombing in World War II (again, people will differ over how necessary that was). From the Middle Ages on, Germany was at the forefront of European culture. Her abbeys, cathedrals, and universities were renowned from the Atlantic to the Urals.

Moreover, the Germans traditionally spoke about freedom as much as do modern-day Americans. In 1789, there were over three hundred states in Germany, ranging from great powers like

Habsburg Austria and Hohenzollern Prussia, to tiny micro-lordships only a few miles across—each of which could mint its own money and charge its own taxes, tolls, and customs. Many of these were Imperial Free Cities, owing allegiance to no lord but the Holy Roman Emperor himself. Should a serf make his way into one of these, and remain for a year and a day, all obligations owed his own feudal lord were absolved. Thus was coined the old German proverb, *Stadtluft macht frei*: "City air makes one free."

But this love of freedom on the part of nobleman, city, and peasant alike often resulted in anarchy, as the ages wore on from the time of Charlemagne, and the Holy Roman Emperor became ever more a figurehead. As lords and their lands grew in number, so did their castles. Some of these noblemen, less scrupulous than their neighbors, used their keeps as headquarters for plundering expeditions. These were the famous "robber barons." But even honest counts and barons were quite likely to wage war on their neighbors. The sorts of private tragedies and scandals we have become familiar with in this book were rife in these places.

When Luther began his revolt against the Church, some of the peasants took him at his word and revolted against their feudal masters. Although Luther himself called on them to submit to the nobility (and on the latter, to slaughter their rebellious serfs), the stage was set for a tremendous amount of bloodshed, culminating in the Thirty Years War of 1618 to 1648. Many a ruined castle and its resident specter date from this time.

Indeed, from this era forward, the fertile German imagination peopled its literature with all sorts of spooks—a word, incidentally, derived from the German *Spuk*, even as "ghost" comes from *Geist*. Of course, medieval German writing had a lot of this stuff as well, and then as now the sorts of festivals referred to earlier—particularly Walpurgis Nacht and Saint John's Eve—have been well and thoroughly celebrated in Germany. Certain areas of the country, such as the Black Forest, the Harz, the Taunus, the Spessart, and the Rhine Valley are particularly legend-ridden.

The efforts of the Germans to free themselves from the French conquerors led by Napoleon began another burst of rhetoric about freedom, as well as the artistic revival we call Romanticism (not surprisingly, both in writing, composing, and in painting, the Romantics of all nationalities went in heavily for supernatural themes). But the course of the nineteenth century saw Germany unified politically through the ejection of the genial Habsburgs in favor of the more militaristic Hohenzollerns of Prussia. This in turn led to the building up of an efficient state apparatus which— the moderating effect of the Hohenzollerns removed after World War I—was put to use by Adolf Hitler in ways too well known for us to focus on here. Suffice it to say that for many, Germany and the Nazis became a symbol of overwhelming evil. (Although to be fair, Stalin and the Soviets far exceeded their rivals in murder as far as sheer body count goes, and Mao Tse-tung and his successors managed to top both of them put together. But of course, victory counts for much in the public esteem.)

At any rate, the ghosts of the past lay heavily upon the German psyche, as well as on the minds of those foreigners who are connected with the country. Forgotten is the fact that there are more Americans of German descent than of English, and that large numbers of Germans established progressive colonies in Canada, Australia, New Zealand, South Africa, Namibia, and Latin America. They were responsible for revolutionizing trade and agriculture in those countries.

Lovers of Tsingtao beer owe their favorite beverage to German brewers, while German vintners in the Barossa Valley of South Australia laid the foundations of that state's wine industry. These settlers brought their own stories of ghosts and goblins to their new lands. Anyone who has driven through Pennsylvania Dutch country, and felt a chill looking at the ubiquitous hex signs there, should know that they are gazing upon the purest medieval German magic. Imagine what lies in store for you at the haunted castles and palaces of the Fatherland itself!

The Once and Future Ghost?

One of the most famous haunted palaces in Europe may not exist anymore, although it might do so again one day. This is the famous Berliner Schloss, the Hohenzollern Castle in the middle of Berlin, which was dynamited by the Communists in 1950. First built as a medieval-style castle in 1443 by the Hohenzollern electors of Brandenburg, the *Stadtschloss* ("City Castle") underwent many changes until 1699. In that year, although construction would not finish until the mid-nineteenth century, it began to be transformed into the Baroque palace that remains alive in yellowing photographs, and in the memories of older Germans.

The palace echoed the history of its owners, as they expanded their small and unproductive state into the kingdom of Prussia (a feat achieved by Friedrich I in 1713, the same year as the duke of Savoy, Vittorio Emmanuele II, managed to gain the royal title). Successive Hohenzollerns—most notably Friedrich II, called "Frederick the Great"—turned Prussia into a first-rate European power. By 1815, it ranked as one of the big five, alongside Great Britain, France,

Austria, and Russia. With the acquiescence of Wilhelm I, Otto von Bismarck defeated the Habsburgs in 1866 (thus eliminating their centuries-old predominance in Germany) and dominated the remaining German states. This led to the proclamation of the German Empire in 1871. In 1888, Wilhelm II became kaiser, with later results that are known to all. Less was heard about his endowment of Harvard University's Busch-Reisinger Museum in 1905.

In any case, the Berliner Schloss became ever more lavish as its owners became more powerful. But even as they went from triumph to triumph (with a few temporary defeats mixed in, most notably at the hands of Napoleon), the family and its Stadtschloss lived with—and concealed—a strange and eerie secret. This was the White Lady of the Hohenzollerns, or the family ghost.

There are different theories as to who she might be, but the wise old folk of Berlin have always held that she is the ghost of Anna Sydow, a beautiful widow. She became the mistress of the elector, Joachim II (1535–1571). Joachim was a character not unlike Henry VIII, although he drew the line at serial marriages. In the ferment of the Protestant revolt, he emulated Henry in breaking with the Pope and taking over the government of the Church (as well as the property of the monasteries). But again like Henry, he insisted that actual doctrines remained unchanged. To the scandal of his subjects, he gave his mistress many honors. On his deathbed, Joachim made his son, Johann Georg, promise to retain the Church order he had inaugurated and to keep Anna well maintained. After his father's death, Johann ordered the Church in Brandenburg to accept Calvinism, and flung Anna into prison at Spandau fortress. There she dwelt for the rest of her life.

Just before Johann Georg came to die, a female apparition was seen wandering the halls of the castle at night. Dressed in white and wearing a widow's veil and black gloves, she smelled of the grave, and frightened the servants who saw her out of their wits. In the morning, their master was dead. From that time on, her appearance announced the death of a family member. She appeared regularly at such occasions, most notably in 1659, when Elector Johann Sigismund passed on. But seven years after that, she put in an unrelated appearance.

Since by this time the White Lady's visits were legendary, the servants in the Berliner Schloss constantly talked about her. The chamberlain of the castle, second only to the elector himself (in those days, the so-called "Great Elector," Friedrich Wilhelm, who incorporated East Prussia into Brandenburg) in the palace hierarchy, scoffed at what he regarded as mere downstairs superstition. One night, having previously drunk a great deal and expressed the wish that he should see her, the chamberlain bade his master good night and descended the great staircase.

As he did so, he saw the White Lady ascend toward him. Emboldened by drink, he shouted at her, "You old creature! You have not drunk enough blood yet; do you want to get still more?" At that, she grabbed him by the neck and threw him down the stairs. The Great Elector, hearing the commotion, sent a pair of pages with candles to see what the matter was. No one was to be seen except the chamberlain lying at the bottom of the stairs. Although he had suffered nothing worse than a few cracked ribs, he became a fervent believer in the White Lady ever after. From that time on, moreover, those who met her and greeted her politely received a decorous nod of the head in return, although she never spoke.

The White Lady soon returned to her more familiar task. One year after the chamberlain episode, the Great Elector's first wife, Luise Henriette, stepped into the royal bedroom and saw the White Lady sitting at her desk. Sure enough, the electress died soon after. Another such visitation occurred just before her husband died in 1688. When the castle was being further renovated in 1709, the skeleton of a woman was found hidden in a wall. Presuming it to be Anna, Friedrich I ordered it buried with proper rites in the graveyard of the Berliner Dom, in hopes that this would lay the ghost to rest. It was no help, for she appeared again, in her black gloves, before he himself died three years later.

She reappeared before the death of Friedrich Wilhelm I in 1740, and several times during the winter of 1796 and 1797. In rapid succession there perished the Crown Prince's brother, Prince Ludwig, on December 28; the king's mother, wife to Friedrich II followed; and at last, Friedrich Wilhelm II died. In the year 1840, Friedrich Wilhelm III was already fearful, given that—save in 1540—a Hohenzollern had died in every year with a forty in it. Sure enough, the White Lady put in an appearance, and the king was soon laid beside his ancestors in a tomb in the crypt of the Berliner Dom.

But as the years passed by, Anna's bitterness against the family (if indeed she ever felt any—it might be argued that alerting a person to their impending death is something of a kindness, giving them the chance to prepare) had waned. She began fulfilling other tasks, apart from death warnings.

When court festivities were due to begin, if any doors, windows, and locks rattled by themselves around the palace, it was a sure sign of social success. On the other hand, if a servant was lazy, or dishonest, or had blasphemed, he was likely to find himself pushed around by unseen hands, pelted with rocks from nowhere, or shrieked at by a disembodied voice. Most touching of all, however, was the White Lady's concern for the royal children. If a nanny forgot herself so much as to fall asleep in the nursery, and then woke up suddenly, she was likely to see the ghost standing bent over a princely infant's cradle, or even rocking the little one in her ghostly arms—without, of course, the telltale black gloves.

Whether or not she appeared before the death of Friedrich Wilhelm IV in 1861, or Wilhelm I and Friedrich III in 1888, this writer does not know. Already, the cutting-edge Hohenzollerns had a modern publicity department in place, to cushion them somewhat from the world. When Wilhelm II died in 1941, he was an exile in the Netherlands. Who is to say what the Nazi guards at the palace saw? In 1950, the Communists, as mentioned, destroyed the Berliner Schloss, so the death of the Kaiser's grandson, Louis Ferdinand, a few years ago went unheralded.

But, in 1989, soon after the fall of the Berlin Wall, talk immediately began about rebuilding the old Stadtschloss, which was, after all, the center of Berlin. Unter den Linden's beautiful palaces were designed to lead the visitor to Stadtschloss. Now the venue goes to an empty lot. In 1993, a plastic tent was erected on the site, containing an exhibit on the palace. This spurred interest in the idea of rebuilding the castle, and a few years ago the Bundestag authorized the plan, although it is to be funded by private donations. Construction is due to begin in 2005, with an expected completion date of 2010. While the many rooms once occupied by servants and the like will be given over to other uses, the state apartments will be restored. The visitor will be able to pass through them, each Baroque chamber more splendid than the last, and culminating finally in the resurrected glory of the throne room.

All of which brings up an important question, suggested at the beginning of this account: When the Berliner Schloss is rebuilt, will the White Lady return? Or would she insist that the young crown prince, Georg Friedrich, reoccupy that glittering throne room before she deigns to come back? One cannot tell, of course, until and unless either or both of those things happen. But she would surely appreciate any donations you make to her home's restoration. And if you find yourself, one dark night, looking over the construction site in downtown Berlin, show no fear if she appears to you. It is not your family's deaths she foretells. If you greet her politely, she may well favor you with a nod.

Berliner Schloss Foundation

Tel: + 49 (0) 4532 40 41 12
Fax: + 49 (0) 4532 40 41 33
http://www.berliner-schloss.de/

Happily Invisible

The Rhine Valley is filled with strange tales—dragons, mermaids, and of course, ghosts. Typical of the haunted castles along the great river is Reichenstein, a fortress whose history extends back almost a thousand years. At that time, the site belonged to the great Imperial Abbey of Kornelimunster, who had received the area almost two hundred years before as a gift from the Emperor Louis the Pious, the son of Charlemagne.

The abbot in turn farmed the castle out to a lay administrator— a bailiff. This position was often hereditary. Just as often, despite their nominal employers' oft-repeated orders, these bailiffs turned "robber knights." Exasperated, the Archbishop of Mainz raised an army and took the castle, leveling it to the ground. The resident bailiff, Philipp von Hohenfels, promised future good conduct in return for his life. Instead, he rebuilt Reichenstein stronger than before and soon returned to his old ways.

This took place during the time of the "Great Interregnum," but when Rudolf von Habsburg was elected emperor in 1273, he began a campaign of ejecting the robber knights from their castles. It was Reichenstein's turn in 1282. After some pitched battles and a siege, the forces of order prevailed for a short time, although the master of the place, Dietrich von Hohenfels, was eventually beheaded and his henchmen hanged. The castle was yet again destroyed, and once more rebuilt.

Over the centuries, it passed through various hands, at last being restored by a noble family in the late nineteenth century. After World War II, the family ran it as a museum, before selling it to Egon Schmitz in 1987. He in turn has opened it to the public as a hotel. It is a masterpiece of Gothic and Neo-Gothic architecture, and offers both fine accommodations and several extremely good restaurants.

With its grisly past, it is fitting that the castle enjoys a ghost, who is heard and felt rather than seen. Many guests have complained that they do not feel alone, and doors and windows open of their own accord. While such activities may seem run-of-the-mill (save to those experiencing them), it is probably just as well that no dramatic apparitions take place, given the probable appearance of the being that would materialize.

He is believed to be Dietrich von Hohenfels, the robber knight defeated by Rudolf von Habsburg. After his defeat, von Hohenfels begged the victorious emperor not to save his own forfeited life but to spare his nine sons. But Rudolf, well aware that the youths had studied robbing, looting, rapine, and murder with a master, and wanting to deter all other robber knights, refused the errant knight's request. He declared, however, that he would let God judge.

Von Hohenfels's guards led him and his sons to the emperor's judgment seat, on the current site of the nearby St. Clement Chapel. The sons were lined up in a row. Rudolf declared, "Look, you murderer, here are all your sons. In a moment your head will roll into the sand, but should you manage to walk past your brood [headless], I will keep every one of them alive whom you manage to pass." Their father looked every one of them in the eye, and then gazed at the path he must walk, were he to save them.

Moments later, the robber knight's head was struck from his body with one stroke. But instead of collapsing, he swayed a little, and walked by each of his sons, one by one. This task accomplished, he fell to the ground. Blood spurted into the air from the stump of his neck and sprayed the witnesses. True to his word, the emperor pardoned the nine, and then left. On the site, relatives of the executed prisoner built the still extant St. Clement Chapel, in order for Masses to be said for the deceased.

Interestingly enough, Victor Hugo visited the castle—at that time, still in ruins. As he explored it, he made a discovery: "As I walked along my glance fell onto a corner of a gravestone which emerged from the rubble. Quickly I bent down. I removed the mud with hands and feet and in a few moments I had uncovered a very lovely tomb plate from the fourteenth century. It was made of red Heilbronn sandstone. On this plate lay a knight in armor who had no head."

If you visit the castle, and either stay or just view the fascinating museum, you may well hear or feel strange things. But be grateful that you are unlikely to see anything—the sight just might make you lose your head!

Hotel Burg Reichenstein
Im Burgweg 25
D-55413 Trechtingshausen am Rhein
Germany

Tel: +49 6721 6101
Fax: +49 6721 6198
http://rhinecastles.com/hotel-burg-reichenstein/willkommen-
  auf-burg-reichenstein/index.html

Vampire Homeland

The map of Central Europe has altered many times over the centuries. Germans, Slavs, and that mysterious race from central Asia, the Magyars, have all struggled over the countries of this region. From time to time outsiders, like the Mongols and the Ottoman Turks, have played their own damaging role. But out of the welter of blood and horror run two unifying presences: the Holy Roman Empire and the House of Habsburg.

Up until 1918, Habsburgs ruled over all or part of Austria, Hungary, the Czech Republic, Slovakia, Slovenia, Croatia, Poland, Ukraine, Serbia, and Romania. At one time or another, the Habsburgs have also been monarchs of Germany, Italy, Belgium, the Netherlands, Spain, and much of what is now Latin America, as well as the Philippines. The presence of the family's double-eagle badge over the door of the Spanish Governor's Palace in San Antonio, Texas, is a reminder of their once vast sway. We met Rudolf, the first of the family to be Holy Roman Emperor, at Reichenstein. All across their former domains rest castles and palaces which once belonged to them—and a few which still do.

They, however, rarely conquered these vast domains. "Let other nations make war; you, O happy Austria, marry!" was the family motto—and one which seemed about to repeat itself a few years ago, until the present Crown Prince of Belgium married and produced an heir; his sister is married to a Habsburg archduke.

Their original home, Habsburg (originally *Habichtsburg*— "Hawk's Castle") was conquered by the Swiss long ago, and today is a ruin, albeit an impressive one. Despite its name, there are no hawks there today. Local legend claims that the birds vanished after the last Habsburg emperor, Karl I, was deposed at the end of World War I. But many believe that the hawks will only return when the Habsburgs are restored to their rightful place as emperors of the Holy Roman Empire.

Whether or not that prophecy is true, there certainly were, and are, stories of a Habsburg curse, perhaps inspired by the tragic life of Emperor Franz Josef. His brother, Emperor Maximilian of Mexico, was murdered by Juarez in 1867. His son, Rudolf, committed suicide at Mayerling. His beloved empress, Elizabeth, was assassinated in 1898, and the same fate befell his nephew and heir, Franz Ferdinand, in 1914—thus provoking the outbreak of World War I and the end of the empire. He did not live to see this, dying two years after the outbreak.

His nephew, Karl, who succeeded him, tried twice (unsuccessfully) to retake Hungary after being driven off the throne, and was exiled to the island of Madeira where he died. But, as they say, he who laughs last, laughs best. The pious Karl's body being incorrupt, and his miracles having been proved, he was beatified in Rome on October 3, 2004, an honor unlikely to be given his main antagonists, Woodrow Wilson, Lloyd George, and Clemenceau. His son, the Archduke Otto, a longtime European unity activist, fulfilled a lifelong dream that same year of seeing

Hungary, the Czech Republic, Slovakia, and Slovenia join Austria in the European Union.

But the Habsburg lands were traditionally difficult to govern. Filled with a crazy-quilt of peoples whose mutual history had led them to cordially dislike one another, they would show, after 1918, just what that hatred could do if allowed to run amok. Each has an exceedingly strange folklore of their own. To the regulation ghosts, witches, and fairies, they add the werewolf—and above all, the vampire.

One way the Habsburgs dealt with their hot-blooded subjects was to impose a neutral and often incurably dull bureaucracy upon them. In their reports to various government departments in Vienna are sometimes found hair-raising tales of vampirism and such, related in the same bland language used to relate stories of tax collection and road repair. The celebrated tale of the vampire Arnold Paul is one such story.

Paul was a soldier who, in 1727, returned from war to his village near Belgrade, then under the Habsburg sway. Paul used the money he had saved from the army to buy a cottage and an acre or two of land. Despite being popular with his neighbors and considered to be very honest, he had a certain wariness about him that had not been present when he left. When Paul married, his new wife asked the reason for his unease. He explained that while fighting in Greece, his unit had been assigned to an area renowned for its vampires. One of these had attacked him. It was in its grave, whence he and his fellows removed and destroyed it. He resigned from the army and fled to his village.

Nothing untoward happened for some time. But then he fell from a haycart, was killed, and duly buried. About a month afterwards he began to appear to various people at night, and some of these observers sickened and died. After enduring his depredations through a cold winter, the villagers appealed to the imperial authorities in Belgrade, who sent two military officers and three army surgeons to investigate. It is from their official report, dated January 7, 1732, that we have the tale.

The group exhumed Arnold Paul's body, as well as all of those who had died during the winter. Paul's body and four of the others were found to be whole, entire, and full of blood. The report dispassionately recounts how the five corpses were staked and burned, and that Paul's gave out a shriek as he was impaled. Although this action seemed to cure the problem, six years later it broke out again in the village, and was dealt with similarly.

In such remote provinces as Bukovina and Transylvania, the end of the nineteenth century found the major cities adorned with *Jugendstil* architecture, the central European version of *Art Nouveau* imported directly from Vienna's Ringstrasse, while the remoter countryside still treasured darker beliefs of the past. Scattered here and there were the palaces and castles of the nobility, many of which came equipped with strange tales of their own. Here are a few of them.

The Greatest Hungarian Ghost

The Széchenyi clan is one of the most illustrious Hungarian noble families. Typical of their class, however, they have a lot of foreign blood, being in fact descended in one branch from Mary Queen of Scots. Their beautiful, ancestral mansion lies in the far west of Hungary, and achieved its present appearance under the ownership of the nineteenth-century Count István Széchenyi, called by his admiring countrymen the "Greatest Hungarian." The crypt of the mausoleum where he is entombed on the property bears the following motto over the entrance: WE WERE AS YOU ARE NOW, AND YOU WILL BE AS WE ARE NOW. Even today, thousands of Hungarians visit his tomb every year.

The reason is not difficult to discover. In his lifetime István was a real pioneer. He was responsible for the building of the Széchenyi Bridge in downtown Budapest, and also for the construction of a university, a library, and numerous other civic improvements. A nobleman proud of his station in life, he called on his colleagues to invest heavily in the newly born industries of the day. He felt that they should deal paternally with their workers, as they did with their peasants. It was his great fear that otherwise, mere wealth would dominate the factories, the workers would be mistreated, and social unrest would be the result.

Moreover, István was an active participant in the tumult of his time. Despite his deep loyalty to the Habsburgs, he joined the revolutionary government of 1848 in hopes of moderating its course. In this he failed, and as he had feared, the revolt was crushed, and the country subjected to a painful period of occupation.

One night in 1860, he returned to his home at Nagycenk from a stay at the sanitarium in Doebling, Austria. His majordomo greeted him, had the drawbridge lowered, and bade a stable hand to bring his horse to the stable. All the servants who were awake were happy to see the count return home. The senior servant then accompanied his master up to his office, and lit a kerosene lamp for him. Wishing him good night, the majordomo went to bed. The next morning, however, the master's bed was empty. The lamp was still lit in the office, and his horse was not in the stable. Just then, word arrived that István had killed himself at Doebling the night before.

The count has never been seen since in his old home, part of which is now a museum dedicated to him (the other part a hotel). But who knows? Perhaps you may catch a glimpse!

Széchenyi House
Kiscenki út 3
9485—Nagycenk (Györ-Moson-Sopron)
Hungary

Museum
Tel: +36 (0) 99 360 023
Fax: +36 (0) 99 360 260

http://www.museum.hu/nagycenk/szechenyi
http://szechenyi.gymsmuzeum.hu
E-mail: szechenyi.nagycenk@museum.hu
E-mail: nagycenk@gymsmuzeum.hu

Hotel
Tel: +36 (0) 99 360 061
Fax: +36 (0) 99 360 061

The Alchemist's Lair

Prague Castle was begun at the end of the nineteenth century. Successive kings added to its might, and it became (as it still is) the depository of the Bohemian crown jewels. The kings of Bohemia became electors of the Holy Roman Empire. As might be expected, some won the coveted goal for themselves. One of these was the fourteenth-century ruler, Charles IV, the first emperor to make Prague his major residence. Much of the present-day castle and city owe their appearance to him. In 1526, the Habsburgs inherited the place, and in 1600 it became the residence of Rudolf II, Holy Roman Emperor, King of Hungary, and, of course, King of Bohemia.

Unlike his predecessors, however, Rudolf was interested in alchemy rather than warfare. He surrounded himself with practitioners of that art, as well as other arcane disciplines. Under his rule, Prague Castle became a citadel of the bizarre. He also built a menagerie of exotic animals, to match, perhaps, the equally exotic people who thronged his court. Magicians, cabalists, and astrologers—all were welcome.

But the court of Rudolf was not the only odd scene the castle has witnessed. Imperial emissaries have been thrown out of windows, sieges have been withstood, and crowds have gone delirious with joy at coronations. All of these events seem to have left their mark. Today, as a result, locals will warn you about any number of ghosts. If you enter the royal crypt, you are likely to encounter Charles IV's four successive wives. They will be too busy fighting among themselves and looking for their husband to bother with you, however.

On one side of the castle walls is the Jeleni trench. There the visitor may encounter the ghost of an old man, who, during the reign of Rudolf II, made "remedial" oils and ointments, potions and simples. He died unnoticed in the trench, and one of the Imperial menagerie attendants decided to use the unattended corpse as extra food for his carnivores. Apparently, the old man did not appreciate this treatment. He returned to haunt the keeper, driving him to madness and finally, to hanging himself. Meeting him today is considered a sign of impending doom.

Prague continues to exert a magical hold on its visitors. Perhaps this comes from lingering alchemical influences. But whatever the reason, you may well find the castle too haunting to leave—certainly others have.

Prague Castle
Castle Hill
Prague
Czech Republic

Tel: +420 224373368
http://old.hrad.cz/index_uk.html
E-mail: frantisek.kadlec@hrad.cz

Ghosts of the Rising Sun

Asia is a world apart from the West, and the roots of this difference lie squarely in the supernatural. With our ever-increasing secularism, we tend to forget how much of our cultural and social attitudes are a direct result of religion. The followers of the three great monotheistic religions do not divinize the natural world as others do, because they do not see gods in every natural phenomenon, and they have a different view of human relations and family life, because they do not worship their ancestors. Christian nations have a very specific view of the physical world, because of the idea of the Incarnation, the Catholic doctrine of the Sacraments, which has had a powerful influence on countries where that faith has, or did, predominate. Moreover, this religious influence is true regardless of the level of conscious belief in these faiths.

So too in Asia, outside the Islamic or Christian areas. For in Christianity and Islam, with death comes the judgment; thus ghosts are beheld with a certain ingrained attitude of caution. But in South and East Asia, where belief in reincarnation is prevalent, ghosts are often seen as beings that are simply on their way to some other state. Ancestor worship, moreover, implies that family specters may be on their way to becoming divinities in their own right, and the bad phantoms among them may become demons.

Certainly, where ghosts are looked at in the West as exceptional phenomena, in the East, they are seen as normal, more or less. Often, however, they are regarded with terror, and consequently, many ingenious methods have been developed to foil them. Witness *feng shui*. Thought of as a method of bringing good luck via landscaping and architecture, feng shui is actually a way of preventing evil spirits from bringing ill fortune. So fear-inducing are these evil spirits that even well-educated people alter their lives accordingly.

In 1935 Ananda Mahidol became king of Thailand. A ten-year-old schoolboy in Switzerland at the time of his accession, he remained there throughout World War II. This was probably just as well, given that "his" government had allied itself with Japan. Returning to Thailand in late 1945, he was mysteriously murdered in the Grand Palace by a gunshot wound to the head in 1946. His younger brother, Bhumibol Adulyadej, assumed the throne. But, supposedly as a result of his brother's death there, His Majesty still refuses to live in the Grand Palace.

But such beliefs affect time as well as space. Under the influence of Taoism and Buddhism, the Chinese celebrate several festivals honoring—and placating—the dead. *Qingming*—meaning "clear brightness"—is a springtime observance, similar to the Christian Easter in some ways. The Chinese celebrate the new season, planting, and the rebirth of nature after winter. Observed two weeks after the vernal equinox, the time in the Western calendar is between April 4 and 6. Traditionally, eggs were boiled, colored, and then broken. People hung willow branches on their windows, and the emperor planted trees.

Today, however, Qingming is given over to venerating dead ancestors. Honoring the dead is one of many ways good Confucians demonstrate filial piety. Families go to graveyards to visit their family plots, and offer their dead relations dried mushrooms, bean curd, noodles, and steamed buns and cakes. They then eat the offerings themselves, weed the graves, clean the tombstones, and decorate them with flowers. Paper gifts in the shape of houses and cars are burned as offerings to the dead, in the belief that these gifts will be real in the afterlife.

But there is another celebration for the dead: the Festival of Hungry Ghosts. (Occurring in the seventh month of the lunar calendar, it was August 16 to September 13 in 2004.) According to Chinese belief, ghosts who have no families to venerate them are allowed to return to earth during this time. The wraiths of suicides and murderers are particularly feared, as they had no one to bury them or perform the requisite rites. It is believed that at this time they return to the scenes of their death, intent on wreaking havoc on the living.

Although the rulers of Communist China suppressed the festival, it is celebrated with great gusto in Singapore, Hong Kong, and among the Chinese diaspora. Believing that these ghosts are often vengeful, the point of the festival is to placate them with food and money. Since the latter means the burning of paper currency, many use special fake notes instead. Special banquets are prepared for the hungry ghosts. Swimming is taboo, for fear that an evil ghost might drown the swimmer. Children are encouraged to come home early each night, for fear that a ghost might possess them.

On the fifteenth day of the festival, sumptuous feasts are prepared for family ghosts, and Buddhist and Taoist priests chant liturgies, perform rituals, and offer incense, paper money, and food to the ghosts. Although these clerics celebrate the same festival at the same time, they all do so in different ways.

Japan, having taken so much of its culture from China, has also adapted the Hungry Ghosts festival, which in Japanese is called

Obon. Shinto, the local religion, teaches, amongst other things, that the dead may themselves become minor deities, or *mitama* (the dead who are enshrined and venerated in Shinto shrines). Where Buddhism in China fused with Taoism and Confucianism, in Japan, Shinto became its partner. Obon exemplifies this connection.

Lanterns are hung outside of houses to guide the ancestors' spirits, obon dances (*bon odori*) are performed, graves are visited, and food offerings are made at house altars and temples, just as in Chinese areas. In the hot summer nights, ghost stories are told. Floating lanterns are set off into rivers, lakes, and the ocean to guide the ghosts back to their own world at the end of the festival.

As with China, Japan originally used the lunar calendar, switching to the solar version after the Meiji Restoration in 1867. Since Obon had fallen in the seventh month of the old calendar, many Japanese communities began to observe it in July. Others, seeing that the direct correlation of the lunar year's seventh month is August, celebrate it then. There are innumerable local variations in customs as well as times of celebration. At the end of Obon, bonfires are built to send the ghostly visitors back to the beyond. This is an important task, but apparently not always successful. In fact, the country is rife with tales of hauntings and possessions. Some of these spirits are demonic, which is reflected in the Japanese word *obake*, meaning either "monster" or "ghost."

While the obake are feared, the mitama are seen as allies and protectors of the living. Even so, for the Westerner, the most ominous of these places must be the shrine called Yasukuni Jinja. Here are enshrined the mitama of all those Japanese servicemen who lost their lives fighting for their country and emperor—particularly in World War II.

Of course, the priests of Yasukuni Jinja have a very different view of the war than do most of us in the West. According to one Yasukuni commentator, "Japan's dream of building a Great East Asia was necessitated by history and it was sought after by the countries of Asia." Of the soldiers venerated there, the same writer adds, "With heartfelt thoughts for the increasing prosperity of generations and generations to come of their families, relatives, and their fellow countrymen, these noble souls endured hardships and offered even their lives for the sake of their nation and race." There are two sides to every coin, as the cliché goes. Does Yasukuni represent the ghost of a possibly renascent Japanese Imperialism? That is one phantom sure to strike fear into the hearts of many. Or is this merely a healthy patriotism after the trauma of the country's postwar reconstruction? Testing the spirits requires discernment, to be sure.

At any rate, feudal Japan was literally covered with castles, owned by the *Daimyo*, the territorial nobility, and staffed by the equivalent of knights, the *Samurai*. At the top of the national structure was the military regent, the *Shogun*, centered in Edo (present-day Tokyo), who was the actual ruler of the land. Off in Kyoto was the *Tenno*, the emperor whose ancestors had been relegated to ritualized impotence centuries before. In 1868, however, this all changed with the Meiji Restoration. The emperor emerged from his cocoon, and, at the head of a band of forward-looking leaders, took control of the country.

The new rulers of Japan immediately began to modernize the country. The old nobility were reconstructed as a service elite, the *Kasuko*—or "flower families." Modeled after the British lords, they staffed the upper house of the new Japanese Parliament, the House of Peers. Most of these folk who had owned castles deserted them for modern-style mansions and palaces—hence the sad song, *Kojo no Tsuki* ("A Ruined Castle by Moonlight") which was an elegy for old Japan.

But the new Japan would require an elegy as well, as a result of World War II. The Kasuko were to a great degree impoverished by the land reform imposed by the allies, while the 1948 constitution not only abolished the House of Peers, it took away their titles as well. Most of the remaining castles in Japan today belong to the national, prefectural, or city governments, and the old nobility tend to keep to themselves. Still, like ghosts, they remain a presence. For example, in the quiet seclusion of the old Peer's Club, the *Kasumi Kaikan*, their titles are still used. In some of the old castles of Japan, literal ghosts carry on the old traditions.

Haunting Near the Emperor

The Imperial Palace in Tokyo was originally built on the site of Edo Castle. Around the palace buildings is a large park surrounded by moats and massive stone walls in the center of Tokyo. Edo Castle was the seat of the Tokugawa shoguns, actual rulers of Japan from 1603 until 1867. In 1868, the Tokugawa were overthrown and the Emperor Meiji assumed control, moving from Kyoto to Tokyo. In 1888, the new Imperial Palace was completed on the site of Edo Castle. The palace was destroyed during World War II, but reconstruction started after the war. The structure reached completion in October 1968, and the Imperial Family moved in during April of the following year. The Imperial Palace was rebuilt using traditional Japanese architecture with primarily Japanese materials. It is a steel-framed, two-story building with an underground floor and an inclined roof with long protruding eaves.

As a rule, the palace buildings and inner gardens are closed to the public. But on January 2 (New Year's Greeting) and December 23 (the Emperor's Birthday), visitors are able to enter the inner palace grounds and see the members of the Imperial Family, who make their public appearances on a balcony. The rest of the year, guided tours of the palace are offered in Japanese, with an English pamphlet and audio guide provided by the Imperial Household Agency.

The palace is actually a very busy place, despite its seeming seclusion. Within its walls, many of the ceremonies typical of any monarchy are performed. Here the Emperor swears in the prime minister and chief justice, and ministers of state and other officials are handed their appointments. The emperor confers decorations on the great and the good, and receives foreign ambassadors when they present their credentials. A round of audiences, court luncheons, and state dinners fill out the calendar, alongside the two garden parties held throughout the year. From here the emperor proceeds to the Parliament building to open the Diet.

There are, however, activities peculiar to the emperor of Japan. Traditional Japanese belief states that the emperor is the descendant of the Sun Goddess, Ameratsu. This lineage required him to perform various high priestly rites during the course of the year. While the defeat of the Japanese in World War II and the renunciation of divinity by the current emperor's father ended State Shinto (the established religion which required the paying of divine honors to the emperor), the rituals of the Imperial House (*Koshitzu Shinto*) continued.

The most important of these is *Niinamesai*, the offering to the deities of the first fruits of each year's grain harvest. For this offering, rice is grown in the palace by the emperor himself, and tended by his own hand. Male and female clergy (*Shoten* and *Nai-Shoten*), often drawn from the ranks of the former Kasuko, assist the emperor in the performance of these rites. Many, of course, involve evocation of the Imperial ancestors.

Strange as these goings-on may seem to Westerners, if there are any outright hauntings inside the palace, neither the Imperial

Household Agency, nor the Emperor, nor his clergy are going to tell us. But the immediate neighborhood of the palace is another story. There is a recurrent tale told, much like the "Vanishing Hitchhiker" in the United States, which has apparently happened many times.

According to the story, a man is walking by the wall of the Imperial Palace at a specific point. He sees a pretty girl entirely too close to the edge of the moat. Simultaneously attracted by her form and hoping to rescue her (she is facing away from him), he comes up behind her and warns her of the danger. She turns around—and has no face. (Missing either a face or legs, for some reason, is a recurrent theme in Japanese ghost stories.) He runs away, and ends up next to a nearby noodle cart. He decides to eat something to steady himself, and while slurping his ramen, tells his story to the noodle man. After he finishes, the operator turns around, saying, "Is that so?" He doesn't have a face either, and the man flees. Again, it is a common tale, and almost universally believed by locals, who will tell you it happens frequently.

It is much easier for foreigners to tour the palace than for Japanese, given the Imperial Household Agency's desire to please tourists, and you can make a reservation online. But when you finish, beware of walking around the moat by yourself. There is no telling what you will—or won't—see!

Imperial Household Agency
1-1 Chiyoda, Chiyoda-ku, Tokyo 100-8111
Japan

Tel: +81 3 3213 1111
http://www.kunaicho.go.jp
E-mail: information@kunaicho.go.jp

The Sun Never Sets

The Commonwealth of Nations comprises most of the nations that were formerly a part of the British Empire until its dismantling after World War II. Occupying over a quarter of the world's landmass, the nations of the Commonwealth offer an incredible diversity of peoples, religions, and terrains. But regardless of their differences, they share an enormous institutional and cultural similarity afforded by the shared experience of British rule.

In most of them, legislatures meet with more or less the same pomp as characterizes the "Mother of Parliaments" at Westminster; their armies and navies reflect the spit and polish of the British Army and the Royal Navy; their legal proceedings are conducted in the same manner (and often with all or part of the same costuming) as those of the Old Bailey; their universities and better secondary schools reflect Oxbridge and Eton; and, regardless of the language of the majority, the elites speak, read, write, and often think in English. In a number of these countries, Her

Majesty Queen Elizabeth II remains head of state, although she is represented by a native governor-general. In all of them she is recognized as "Head of the Commonwealth."

Today, this decentralized group is better understood by what it is *not* than by what it is. It is not a political union, as each member state is fully independent of each other, as well as of Great Britain. Neither is it a military alliance nor an economic union. Moreover, its membership divides neatly into two divisions. First, there are the "Old Dominions"—Canada, Australia, New Zealand, and South Africa—to which large numbers of English, Scots, Welsh, and Irish came as settlers, and then, in the case of the first three, outnumbered the natives. Second, there are the countries in the Commonwealth, in which locals remained a majority.

In the latter cases, the gods, ghosts, and demons of the indigenous religions remained a powerful force, even in those sections—such as Uganda and Zambia—where Christianity converted the majority. In the Caribbean islands belonging to the British and primarily settled by slaves, syncretistic religions like Obeah and Pocomania grew up, mixing remnants of the slaves' original beliefs with those of their masters (voodoo, Santeria, and Candomble were similar developments in the French, Spanish, and Portuguese slave-built colonies). With all of these beliefs, ghosts were and are simply part of the milieu, whether one speaks of Bombay, India, or Kingston, Jamaica. "Ghost hunting" in the Western sense is generally left to priests and exorcists in these parts, rather than to scientists or psychics.

In the Old Dominions, however, British attitudes toward these things prevail. Hauntings are seen as something special and out of the ordinary. But the royal palaces and noble castles of the mother country do not exist there. Few titled folk emigrated to the colonies, and most colonials who were ennobled generally went back to Britain. At various times after World War I, the Dominion governments, in an attempt to show their independence, ended the practice of having their locals given titles by the monarch—as though limiting opportunity for advancement somehow forwarded social mobility.

Thus, the castles and palaces to be found in the four countries fall into three basic varieties: the residences of the representatives of the Crown, each usually called "Government House"; military fortifications; and great houses built by the untitled (and, henceforth, untitle-able) aristocracy of the colonies, in emulation of those built at home by folk whom they would like to have considered their peers. As we shall see, buildings in each category underwent dramatic episodes quite capable of producing ghosts as eerie as anything encountered in the keeps of the British Isles.

The settler experience of opening up strange and exotic locales—often in the teeth of opposition by natives whom the new arrivals considered just as strange and exotic—worked powerfully upon the imaginations of the colonials. Although this experience varies, it remains a powerful psychological reality. Little wonder that the works of Sir Rudyard Kipling, considered the foremost apologist for Imperialism, contain many ghost stories.

Whether or not Imperialism was a good thing can and should be debated, but what cannot be argued is that few of the nations of the Commonwealth have been materially or politically better off since independence, and that of all the "-isms" rampant in the twentieth century, Imperialism produced the fewest corpses. Whether or not it produced fewer ghosts is another question.

Maple Leaf Frights

When most of Eastern Canada passed under the British Crown in 1763, the country already possessed two population groups. The first of these were the Indians, called Native Americans south of the border by the more politically correct—although it is a term most of those it refers to do not care for—and First Nations north of it. The various tribes of these folk had their own beliefs, in which often rather frightening ghosts and spirits played an important part. The *Wendigo*, or "soul hunter," would be immortalized by Canadian horror writer Algernon Blackwood, while the *Sasquatch* is of course the northern version of our Bigfoot. Indian legendry would become an important part of Canadian legendry.

The French-Canadians had been arriving in the country since 1608, and had in the succeeding century and a half produced some cultural distinctions of their own. To this day, *Canadiens* or *Quebecois* outside the major cities speak a rather antique French, and many cling to the odd tales referred to in this book's section on France. The Anglo-French duality of Canada would (and does) create a tension, by turns creative and not. But the French-Canadian attitude toward the supernatural remains more European than that of their Anglophone neighbors.

After the conquest of Canada by the British in 1760, however, the settlers from the British Isles brought their own odd beliefs and practices. There are more native speakers of Scots Gaelic in Canada than in Scotland, and here and there in Eastern Ontario there remain out-of-the-way corners where the magical customs of the Highlands still exist. In Newfoundland, which was heavily settled by Scots, Cornish, and Irish, the belief in fairies can still be found.

After the American Revolution, Ontario, New Brunswick, and Nova Scotia received many Loyalist settlers from the States. Determined to remain under the king, these refugees imparted to English Canada as a whole a certain antipathy toward the Americans, one reinforced by the failed U.S. invasions of the country during the War of 1812—a conflict little remembered by Americans, but seen as a mythic event up north.

In addition to the government houses found in Ottawa and most of the provincial capitals, wherein a viceregal figure performs all the tasks that the queen would perform if she lived there, there is a chain of fortifications along the eastern border with the States. Built against invasion from the south, initially garrisoned by British troops, and later by Canadians, these have long since been turned into monuments. Nevertheless, they remain powerful symbols of Canadian nationhood. Haunted figuratively by past events, some also seem to retain actual spirits!

Erie Hauntings

When the British took control of the French possessions in Canada and America's Old Northwest in 1763, they occupied existing French forts along the Niagara River and Upper Great Lakes. Where needed, they constructed new ones; Fort Erie was the first fruit of this effort.

The fort built on the site was erected in 1764, and acted as a supply base for British regulars, Loyalist militia, and Iroquois during the revolution. A new stone fort was begun near the original in 1804, but was not yet finished at the outbreak of war in 1812. Although occupied for a while by the American invaders, the British regained control in November of 1813. It was recaptured by the U.S. on July 3, 1814, and used as a base for the battles of Chippewa and Lundy's Lane. From August until November of that year, the bloodiest fighting ever waged on Canadian soil took place, as the British attempted to retake the stronghold.

Finally, on hearing that the East Coast of the United States was under attack, and with winter coming on, the Americans destroyed the fort and withdrew. The Treaty of Ghent was signed on December 24, 1814, so ending the War of 1812. The British continued to garrison the ruins until 1823. After use as an Underground Railroad terminus and as a base by the Fenians in 1866, the decaying fort became a favored picnic spot, until reconstruction was started in 1937 and completed two years later. It is now an impressive testimony to the bravery of the British and Canadians of almost two centuries ago.

But that legacy continues in more visible, if less tangible, ways. Of the two thousand who died here, there are over 150 men buried on the grounds from both armies. Most famous of the ghosts who have been seen are a woman in the bunkhouse (a photo has been taken of her and has appeared in the local paper), and a soldier in the mess hall. These two ghosts have been seen repeatedly by many of the staff.

During the initial British siege of the fort in 1814, an American soldier was being shaved by one of his comrades when a British cannonball struck. The one doing the shaving lost his hands—but he was the fortunate one. The man he was working on lost his head. The two are seen from time to time walking near the fort—one headless, and the other handless. In a burial pit the skeleton of a decapitated man placed next to one with both arms severed below the elbow were found. Apparently, this discovery did not put the pair to rest.

A ghost wearing a top hat is also sometimes seen in the northwest bastion. Is he a militiaman? Or perhaps he is an Edwardian picnicker reliving a pleasant day in an early summer of the twentieth century? Whoever he may be, you are quite likely to enjoy Fort Erie as an excursion into a past few Americans know about. But you might find that past just a little too close for comfort.

Fort Erie
350 Lakeshore Rd.
Fort Erie, Ontario L2E 6T2
Canada

Tel: (905) 871–0540
http://www.niagaraparks.com/heritage/forterie.php
E-mail: jhill@niagaraparks.com

Ghosts Along Niagara

Fort George stands by Niagara-on-the-Lake, Ontario. The town is one of the most historic in Canada, having been founded by fleeing Loyalists in 1781. It boasts the only lord mayor in Canada, and remains a bastion of Anglo-Loyalist tradition. Across the water on the American side is the old, originally French, Fort Niagara. Because the United States did not compensate the Loyalists as agreed upon in the 1783 Treaty of Paris, the British held on to a number of frontier forts, and Niagara was one of these. After a treaty in 1796, the forces of the Crown withdrew for the disputed posts. Almost immediately they began construction of Fort George. By 1802, it was complete. The new post acted as headquarters for the British army, the local militia, and the Indian Department.

It was an impressive effort, with six earth-and-log bastions linked by a wooden palisade and surrounded by a dry ditch. Inside stood a guardhouse, log blockhouses, a hospital, kitchens, workshops, barracks, officers' quarters, and a stone powder magazine. Like Fort Erie, Fort George was the scene of pitched fighting as control of the area seesawed back and forth between attackers and defenders. Although eventually re-garrisoned, by the 1820s it was falling to ruin. At last, Fort Mississauga and Butler's Barracks replaced it. During the 1930s, Fort George too was restored, and it now stands as a symbol of patriotism and bravery.

This symbolism was bought at a heavy price, however, and the enormous number of ghosts attests to it. There are even regular ghost tours, many of which encounter weird phenomena on their own—so much so that two books have been published by Ghost Tour guide and founder, Kyle Upton, recounting these tales. Upton claims that only three of the buildings are *free* from ghostly activity.

Of the many structures to choose from at Fort George, one that seems especially haunted is the Officers' Quarters, where young unmarried commissioned officers were billeted. As is common among folk of that age, the atmosphere was not unlike that of a college frat house, with all sorts of high jinks and light spirits. It is some of the latter, perhaps, that survive.

Back in August of 1981, major restoration work required the removal of rotting logs from the walls of the Officers' Quarters. This work left large holes, and rendered the building vulnerable to trespassers and vandals. At the request of the fort management, a number of young staff members volunteered to overnight there. Not coincidentally, these employees were roughly the same age as the long-ago British officers who had once lived in the building. Being, like their predecessors, fond of drink, a number of bottles were brought to the impromptu party at the nearby Enlisted Barracks where the volunteers had set out their sleeping bags.

Singing, drinking, and joking duly concluded, the revelers slipped into their respective bags. Almost immediately, banging and crashing noises were heard coming from the Officers' Quarters they were supposed to be guarding. Up jumped the staff. In the senior officers' wing, they found the furniture moved, but nothing damaged. Confused, the lads set about returning the pieces back to their regular positions, and then returned to their sleeping bags. No sooner were they settled in before the noises began again. Once more they leapt out of their bedding, and rushed back to the Officers' Quarters, and once more found the furniture moved. This time, after rearranging the moved objects, they moved their sleeping bags to the sitting room on the opposite side of the building, and prepared to catch the movers. Sure enough, the noises started again, but when the staff ran into the room, they saw the furniture moving by itself.

They all fled outside the fort and into Niagara-on-the-Lake. Ashamed of their fear, and not wanting to abandon their post completely, the staff went to the police station. There, they admitted to the duty officer that they had been drinking, but convinced him nevertheless to return with them. While they waited at the gate, the constable, flashlight in hand, slowly made his way into the darkness of the fort. The young men waited for him to return, and waited, and waited. At last, he came rushing out, shouting at them as he quickly walked to his car, "You didn't see anything in there, and if anyone asks, I've never seen you guys in my life!"

Most of the activities at the fort are not so frightening, but there are quite a few of them. Upton estimates that on about 60 percent of the tours, *something* happens. So Fort George offers a lot of chances for encounters with the unseen. But remember, if you're American, not to make any anti-British or Canadian remarks. After all, you never know who or what will hear!

Niagara National Historic Sites
Box 787, 26 Queen Street
Niagara-on-the-Lake, Ontario L0S 1J0
Canada

Main Voice Mail: (905) 468-4257
Fax: (905) 468-4638
http://www.niagara.com/~parkscan
E-mail: ont-niagara@pc.gc.ca

Ghost Tours of Niagara
http://66.194.153.32/~ghrs/ghosttours/

Her Majesty's Phantom Servant

As mentioned earlier, the name "Government House" is generally the label given to buildings that house the representative of the queen in a given national or provincial capital, in Canada and the rest of the Commonwealth. In Canada, Government House, Ottawa (also called Rideau Hall), is home to the governor-general, who acts in the place of the queen on the national level. But each of the provinces has a similar figure at the head of the government called the lieutenant governor. Although, like his sovereign, the LG is bereft of actual power, he carries out a number of critical ceremonial and social functions. Above all, he is responsible for seeing that his province has a government and premier capable of commanding a majority of seats in Parliament. Again, like the queen and the governor-general, he possesses "reserve powers," the rarely used right to act on his own initiative to preserve the constitution and public order. Other than that, however, all of his political actions must be carried out on the advice of the premier.

Built in 1889, the Government House in Regina saw its first viceregal tenant in 1891. From then until 1945, it was occupied by a series of lieutenant governors. After serving in a variety of capacities between 1945 and the early 1980s (including a veterans rehab center), in 1984, the lieutenant governor's working office returned to Government House. Architecturally, it is a grand mansion filled with a collection of late-Victorian styles and many antiques, built to impress the visitor with the greatness of the Crown.

A large domestic staff assisted the lieutenant governors when they lived here; the current viceregal office is located in the old servants' quarters. For Americans unversed in such things, it is always a bit odd to find a bit of Imperial glory out on the prairie. In addition to housing the present LG's office, the building also encompasses a museum housing the old state apartments and private rooms of former viceroys. In both purpose and appearance, Government House, Regina is a true palace.

As with so many palaces we have seen, it is haunted. Staff members have nicknamed the thing that prowls by night, stomping around on the hardwood floors and flushing toilets, giving him the absurdly inoffensive name "Howie." They think that he is the ghost of a Chinese cook, Cheun, who died in the house in 1938. As mentioned, the lieutenant governor's present offices used to be the servants' quarters, where Cheun lived. Inanimate objects take on lives of there own: a plant falls off a stand in an empty room; a music box plays in the nursery wing; and a pot moves unaided in the former kitchen. The ghost is known to stomp around on the back stairs as well.

"Government House is haunted. There's no doubt in my mind," says Lloyd Begley, curator of Government House Museum. "Ever since his death, there have been strange happenings. For example, Cheun wore a distinctive pair of slippers when he was alive, and people began to hear him walking throughout the house. In the wee hours they'd hear it in the kitchen. They'd hear his footsteps all the time."

Begley has not heard them himself, to be sure. But he has seen and heard other things. "My first experience was in the nursery. I was doing some conservation work in the dining room when I heard the music box in the nursery right above me start to chime, and footsteps down the hallway about sixty feet that just came to an end. I was the only person in the museum." Moreover, some members of the staff have felt a "two- or three-second blast of chill, like something walked past you, or through you," maintains Begley. He says further that he's heard the four-second wail of a baby in the basement when the house was empty.

One staff member saw a man standing in the kitchen, who then vanished, while invisible children have been heard laughing in the empty house. One cleaning lady heard footsteps making their way from the morning room, through the bedroom, to the far wall of the bedroom, and then coming to an abrupt stop. It turned out that behind the wall there was once a bathroom.

Begley sums up the situation this way: "I've been asked if it makes sense for myself to get a parapsychologist in and run some tests, but then you have to ask yourself, do you really want to know? Do you really want to know if the place you go to every morning at eight o'clock is haunted? I don't."

Whatever the case may be, it is comforting, in a sense, to think that one servant's loyalty may last beyond the grave. No matter how updated both Government House and the viceregal position may become, "Howie" won't change. A visit to the place shall certainly expand your view of government. It may do the same for your sense of reality!

Government House
4607 Dewdney Avenue
Regina, Saskatchewan S4P 3V7
Canada

Tel: (306) 787–5773
http://www.iaa.gov.sk.ca/govhouse/

Haunting Down Under

The first British settlers to come to Australia in 1788 were confronted by a world far beyond their ken. While their predecessors in America, 180 years before, found animals and foliage vaguely like their own, the soldiers and convicts sent to Botany Bay were dropped down into a world utterly unlike Europe. The plants were odd, and the marsupial animals were odder. Moreover, while the American Indians were quite strange, after a while their tribal organization played an important part in inter-European rivalries; their values, though alien, were not incomprehensible.

In sharp contrast, the Aborigines in Australia, with their stories of the "Dream Time," their lack of any organization above the clan, and their total dearth of technology seemed a different order of being. Above all, as any European or American who has traveled to the southern hemisphere can attest, the continual sight of stars in the night sky so different to the ones at home give the fleeting impression that the traveler has arrived on a different planet.

Nevertheless, the convicts and free settlers who came to Australia did their best to make their new home as much like the old as they could. Australia's cities and towns boast some of the finest Victorian and Art Deco architecture anywhere in the world. Despite the best efforts of republicans, the governor-general and the state governors, at least for the moment, continue to represent the queen in their respective Government Houses. The educated accent (now somewhat looked down upon) is very reminiscent of Oxbridge, while the more common one reminds the visitor of the cockney from which it partly descends. Despite all the best attempts of intellectuals, media moguls, and politicians in recent years to create a synthetic Australian identity completely separate from Britain, no one really believes they have had much success thus far, so well did the founders and settlers of the country establish their foundations.

But despite all the obvious hints of British influence, Australia remains a very different place for the reasons mentioned. During the nineteenth century, doubtless as a result of the stress between the familiar and the exotic that played out in the everyday life of the country, the ghost story became an important genre of Australian literature. It is little shock that the best-known song the country has produced, *Waltzing Matilda*, even contains an element of the supernatural, with the ghost of a swagman who has plunged into the billabong (or stagnant pool) pledging to return to "waltz matilda."

This is understandable, indeed, given the strangeness the early Australians encountered, and the many stories of hauntings that have come down to us. But as in Canada, there were few titled nobility among the settlers (although many younger sons). Nevertheless, a gentry class did develop, which reveled in building great nineteenth-century houses and estates, many of which survive today. Further, as befitted a rising dominion of the Crown, the viceroys dwelt in ever more splendid Government Houses—quite a jump from the first one, which was merely a tent. In both sorts of buildings, ghosts made their presence felt.

Indeed, despite the best efforts of those who tried to remake the country's identity, the uncanny shall no doubt remain a constant in Australian culture. The lords of media and politics may succeed in creating a sort of ersatz United States, complete with a republic, American spelling, and an utter ignorance of national history—but they will never fish the ghost out of the billabong!

The Blue Lady and Aussie UFOs

Old Government House in the Sydney suburb of Parramatta is Australia's oldest surviving public building, having been built by governors John Hunter and Lachlan Macquarie between 1799 and 1818. As the country residence of the king's representative, it was the acme of early nineteenth-century elegance, and hosts the nation's greatest collection of early Australian furniture as a result. As with any government house, it served as the hub of local social life in old New South Wales, as well as witnessed some of the most dramatic episodes in the early colony's history.

Unfortunately, the completion of the present government house in Sydney in 1845 doomed the building's viceregal career. The cabinet of the self-governing colony informed His Excellency that they would no longer pay for two residences. Although the governor kept the place going at his own expense for an additional two years, when his wife took ill, he gave it up. In 1855, the new governor, Lord Denison, sold all the furniture and fittings at auction.

Old Government House passed through a number of roles (including a fifty-five-year stint in the hands of Australia's most prestigious boarding school, the King's School) until in 1965 it was deeded to The National Trust of Australia (NSW) who have operated it ever since. After three decades of restoration, it was opened to the public.

The building's authenticity is heightened, no doubt, by those past residents who do not leave. Like Fort George, the sheer amount of ghostly activity lends itself to a ghost tour. Many of the employees refuse to stay after nightfall. They may be forgiven, since quite a number of their forerunners, the servants of the nineteenth-century governors, have been seen performing their chores.

Just inside the front gates of Parramatta Park, where the old structure stands, are an obelisk and a tree. Passersby have witnessed apparitions, mysterious white mists, and heard screams. During the restoration of the house, a disembodied face at one of the windows confronted a workman installing a chandelier. Looking in the window to the left, he saw the same face appear again.

For those who have begun to miss the various colored ladies of the British Isles and Europe, it will doubtless be reassuring to know that, at the top of the wooden staircase, the Blue Room is haunted by a Blue Lady. As with the rest of the house, the Blue Room is furnished with such antiques as a four-poster bed and an old wardrobe. On the hallway wall just outside the room is a painting of a young girl named Mary Bligh, who carries a dog in her arms. She matches exactly the description of the Blue Lady, who has been seen stalking the corridor, likewise carrying a dog.

But this visual manifestation outside the Blue Room is not as chilling as what occurs inside. Not only does the wardrobe open by itself, but also quite often it will be found open first thing in the morning. Locking the main door of the room at night does not help either, because sometimes it will open by itself at night, whereas at other times it shows up as open on the security board although it is in reality closed. Staff members have followed people in period clothing (whom they presumed to be reenactors of some sort) into the Blue Room, only to find it empty. Knocks are heard both on the interior and exterior of the door (depending on where the listeners are) by both staff and visitors. There are of course the requisite cold spots and drops in temperature.

On one occasion a guard chatted with a girl dressed in servant attire standing by the table in the dining room. After some amicable conversation, she disappeared in front of him. The same room hosted voices often heard by a former manager. Of course, they would stop as soon as she entered.

These are only a very few of the reported incidents. Old Government House also has the distinction of being the site of the first reported UFO sighting and alien abduction in Australia. Working out in the fields during the early 1800s, a servant saw an "ark" in the sky. He was taken up by it, and later found in a nearby field.

These are just a few of the mysteries waiting to be explored at Old Government House. But perhaps the biggest is how the governors could ever have given up this spot! In any case, you are quite likely to encounter something—or someone—on the tour!

Old Government House
Parramatta Park
Parramatta NSW 2150
Australia

Tel: (02) 9635 8149
http://www.nsw.nationaltrust.org.au/gov.html
E-mail: oghouse@bigpond.com

Ghost Tours
http://www.friendsofogh.com/ghost.html

Kiwi Phantoms

ew Zealand is often thrown together with Australia in the
popular mind—at least, in the mind of those who do not know
either country! What they do have in common is obvious—
British heritage combined with an exotic locale. But the differences
are enormous. A large part of this difference has to do with the native folk the first colonists encountered. The Maori of New
Zealand are Polynesians, and traditionally were among the most
warlike of that race—it took three wars to subdue them. They were
temperamentally better suited to dealing with European society
than were the often seemingly withdrawn Australian aboriginals.
The terrain is quite different as well. In place of the arable coastal
regions and huge arid wastes of Australia, the North and South
Islands of New Zealand offer an enormous range of scenery, from
jungle to high mountain to Norwegian-style fjord.

It has taken the Kiwis, as locals are called, longer to establish a
distinct identity than the Australians—indeed, a large part of it is

that they are *not* Australians. In times gone by the New Zealanders put great stock in the fact that there were no convict settlements in New Zealand, but rather a great many colonization schemes. Such efforts brought the English to Christchurch, the Scots to Dunedin, and the French to Akaroa (albeit in the latter case through the efforts of France, rather than Great Britain). Czechs, Dalmatians, Norwegians, Danes, and Germans all settled in distinct areas, and each brought their own store of folklore. The Maoris had their own as well, of course. For much the same reason as in Australia, ghost stories feature prominently in New Zealand literature. An odd ghost film called *The Frighteners* was a New Zealand production.

As in the rest of the Commonwealth, New Zealand boasts government houses, which operate along the same lines as all the others. In this case there are two, both at the disposal of the governor-general. One is in Wellington, the capital, and the other is in Auckland. But New Zealand society from its foundation was even more egalitarian than Australia's, with a porous class structure. There are only two palaces, and one castle. Fortunately for us, if not its denizens, it is haunted.

Scots Haunting Far from Home

Near the Scots-settled city of Otago rises Larnach Castle. The wealthy merchant and politician, the Honorable William James Mudie Larnach, began its construction in 1871 as a gift for his wife Eliza. For three years more than two hundred workmen constructed the exterior. Master craftsmen brought over from Europe spent twelve more years on the interior. The castle features the finest materials from around the world—Larnach had money to spend, and did so.

This Victorian extravaganza became the luxurious backdrop of a veritable Greek tragedy, because Larnach's wife, Eliza Jane, for whom the place was built, died of apoplexy in the south bedroom at age thirty-eight. Shortly afterwards, Larnach married his wife's sister, but she too died rather early. Larnach's daughter Kate, for whom he built the ballroom, died shortly after her twenty-first birthday. William then tried marriage again, this time with a much younger woman, Constance. She, however, had an affair with her new husband's son, Donald. Disgusted with himself and the situation, the younger Larnach shot himself at the Grand Hotel (now the Southern Cross) in Dunedin. At last, worn out by successive tragedies, betrayals, and the collapse of his business, Sir William followed his son's example, killing himself at his office in 1898.

Since then, the castle has gone through several owners, serving by turns as a family home, a mental hospital, and now, the grandest hotel in the country. But all the comings and goings have not erased the memory of its early tragedies, nor apparently, their supernatural harvest.

The ballroom plays host to Kate Larnach, for whom it was built, and where she appears from time to time. Eliza's presence is felt in the bedroom doorway, near where she died. Doors open by themselves at night, and disembodied footsteps "spook" the staff. On one occasion, when the current owner, Margaret Baker, and the hotel's manager were working late, they heard a heavy piece of furniture being dragged along the floor. Naturally (or supernaturally) nothing was wrong when they checked. Many guests and employees have felt themselves touched by invisible hands on various parts of their bodies.

As might be expected, the sorry story of Sir William Larnach (he was knighted eventually) and his family has made its way into Kiwi literature, specifically into a play entitled *Larnach—Castle of Lies*. It centers on the last half of Sir William's life, his wife and son's affair, his financial woes, and so forth. The Fortune Theater presented the play at the castle's ballroom in 1994, with one hundred invited guests seated in front of a cozy fire.

Apparently, the performance did not make the permanent guests too happy. When the audience began arriving, a storm suddenly started. Smoke from the fireplace blew back down the chimneys, creating an acrid haze that was painful to the eyes. Hail pounded on the roof, making hearing difficult. The temperature dropped, and doors began opening by themselves. When the actor playing

Sir William pulled the trigger at the play's climax, there was a blinding flash of white light—which neither lightning nor special effects had caused. As the castle's current owner says, "The next day all those right-brained businessmen who had been at the play were trying to reconcile what they did or didn't believe with what they had seen and experienced that night."

Innumerable people have experienced bizarre goings-on at Larnach Castle. It is almost comforting to know that New Zealand, which in so many ways emulates Britain more closely than any of the other four "Old Dominions," should also have a haunted keep—and one that is so comfortable and accessible to the public. Should you stay there, keep your eyes open!

Larnach Castle
145 Camp Road, Otago Peninsula
P.O. Box 1350 Dunedin
New Zealand

Tel: + 64 3 476 16 16
Fax: + 64 3 476 15 74
http://www.larnachcastle.co.nz/index.pasp
E-mail: larnach@larnachcastle.co.nz

Springbok Specters

Of the four "Old Dominions," South Africa is in many ways the most distinctive. When the Union of South Africa, bringing together four erstwhile self-governing British colonies—Cape Province, Natal, Orange Free State, and the Transvaal—was launched as an independent nation under the British Crown, it had many of the same appurtenances as the other three. A governor-general presided over the state from his six government houses scattered across the country; a Westminster-style Parliament carried out its work in very similar fashion to that in London; and the universities and secondary schools were very much in the British mold.

But there were very great differences as well. One was that the native population, instead of being decimated, remained a great majority, albeit subservient and disenfranchised. There were also large numbers of Asian Indians and people of multiracial descent (referred to as the "Coloureds" in South Africa today) in a somewhat similar situation. Because of the intense rivalry between the

234

constituent provinces, there was not (and is not) one capital; the prime minister and his cabinet are in Pretoria, the Parliament in Cape Town, and the supreme court in Bloemfontein—each being a different provincial capital.

But the biggest difference was the existence of the Afrikaners. As a total of 60 percent of the white population, these descendants of seventeenth-century Dutch settlers (although there had been Germans and French Huguenots among them) had been conquered by the British in the early nineteenth century. Fleeing British rule in the 1830s for the interior (the so-called "Great Trek"), they had established two independent governments that fought as many wars with the British before being conquered.

As a people with over three centuries in African soil—and thus, loose cultural ties to Europe—they resemble in some ways the French-Canadians, and gave the British much of the same kind of trouble. Eventually, the radical nationalists among them would come to power in 1948, establish the apartheid system of rigid segregation and subjugation of the non-whites, and eventually create a republic free of the Crown in 1961 (Australian republicans, take note!). From then until the introduction of majority rule in 1993, the country underwent increasing isolation from the world community at the insistence of both the United States and Great Britain. Since the end of apartheid, the country has struggled to keep its economy afloat, reconcile the various races and peoples, and stem a rising tide of crime and instability. Viewed dispassionately, these facts do seem to outweigh the benefits. Blacks may live where they want and can now vote; but their incomes and life expectancies have dropped. This is not an argument for apartheid, but it is a sad fact—rather like similar drops in post-Communist countries. No one would want to see Communism restored either, to say the least, but its fall has had a number of unexpected drawbacks.

Despite this unfortunate history, the Afrikaners are an interesting people. In some ways, they have historically been much like the Puritans of our own New England. As rigid Calvinists, they identified with the children of Israel of the Old Testament. They were a people chosen by God. Their arrival—and later, the Trek— was the equivalent of the exodus, and the peoples they encountered were Canaanites. The equivalent of what we call the Puritan work ethic has traditionally been very strong among them, as has a pronounced hostility upon the part of the respectable folk toward drinking, dancing, and the like. One reason why they were so hated by American intellectuals during the apartheid years is that they do give an idea of what Americans might have been like had not massive immigration diluted somewhat the ethos of the Pilgrim fathers.

But just as with the early Puritans, there was and is a weird undercurrent to Afrikanerdom. In the same way that a whole cluster of eerie folk beliefs underlay the Congregationalism of old New England (which flowered at Salem), the same was true at the Cape of Good Hope. One world-famous legend of the Afrikaners is of course that of the "Flying Dutchman," the ghostly square-rigged ship that has haunted the Cape's stormy waters since its captain bet the devil his soul that he could round the Cape safely. He lost, and has been sailing ever since. (Oddly enough, the Dutch in New Amsterdam tell a similar story about one Rambout van Dam, who lost a similar wager to the same gambling partner, and now rows the Tappan Zee—something to think about if you commute into Manhattan!)

But there are many beliefs among the Afrikaners that are less familiar. Although, in the nineteenth century, every Boer home had a Bible, few indeed could actually read it. They were great believers in omens and folk remedies. To treat toothaches, they would lance the swelling and pour the blood into a tree, thus transferring the infection, they believed. From the Zulu and Xhosa peoples around them, they learned such practices as thrusting wounded limbs into the just cut-open stomach of a newly killed goat, and many other remedies of that kind.

"Wise" men and women plied their trade, claiming to sense evil spirits and offering to exorcise them—for a fee. These *Slamaaiers*, as they are called, remain popular in the rural districts. In the pre-apartheid days, African witch doctors were called upon if the Slamaaier could not cure an illness or drive off a demon. But the Dutch Reformed Church disapproved of these practices, and as late as the twentieth century would hold trials for those who resorted to treatment from such folk (the punishment, of course, was excommunication—colonial civil law did not recognize witchcraft as such). The native Black Africans, even today, will sometimes take the law into their own hands and hang a suspected witch.

The Afrikaners were also great believers in second sight and telepathy. Many districts boasted their own clairvoyants, probably the most famous of whom, born with a caul, was Nicolaas van Rensburg, the prophet of Lichtenburg. Born in 1862, van Rensburg was said to have predicted most of the events which afflicted Afrikanerdom in his time, most notably their defeat in the two wars and in the abortive 1914 rebellion.

The Afrikaners also had a great belief in ghosts and other spirits—some of which were obviously derived from African and Malay folklore and religion. The devil remains an active player in Afrikaner belief, often being accused of making personal appearances and of "forcing" people into crimes they would not otherwise have committed.

With such a background, it is small wonder that South Africa offers a large number of ghost tours. And although this country deserves further study, we will visit only one building—the oldest in the country.

Haunted Castle at the Cape

In 1652, Jan van Riebeeck landed at Cape Town's Table Bay with seventy-two men and eight women. Their mission was to set up a way station for the Dutch East India Company ships traveling between the Netherlands and what is now Indonesia. The new arrivals immediately began raising fresh vegetables and other foodstuffs for the company crews. At the same time, they threw up an earthwork fortification. Between 1666 and 1679, this was replaced with the massive stone structure we see today. Its blocks were all brought from the home country. The Castle of Good Hope was both the residence of the governor, his military headquarters, and a place of refuge for the settlers. Even today, it remains the center of the Army for Cape Province (and is depicted on the flags of the South African army, navy, and air force).

In a sense, the castle has played the same role in Cape Town's history as the Tower has in London's. Every weekday, the key ceremony takes place at 10:00 A.M., and the changing of the guard at noon. Having been declared a national monument in 1936, the castle staff does a tremendous job in balancing the building's several uses. It houses the military personnel of the West Cape Department of the army, the famous William Fehr Collection of historic artworks, the Castle Military Museum, and facilities for such traditional Cape regiments as the Queen's Own Cape Town Highlanders and the Duke of Edinburgh's Volunteer Rifles (Cape Town Volunteers).

As headquarters for the colony (a role it retained after the British seized the Cape during the Napoleonic Wars), the governors of the Cape from both countries presided over their governments here. From the Kat Balcony in the inner courtyard (originally built in 1695, then rebuilt in its present form between 1786 and 1790), proclamations and announcements were delivered to the soldiers, slaves, and civilians of the colony. Judicial sentences were read here, and this was where official visitors were welcomed to the castle. In a real sense, after the British conquest, it was the ceremonial heart of the Crown's rule in the country. Had the king ever come to the Cape when the castle was the governor's home, it would have been the royal palace for as long as His Majesty stayed.

With this role, of course, came that of viceregal court; successive governors and their families, retinues, and guards, lived out the drama of their lives against the backdrop of history. Together with the prisoners, soldiers, and all the other denizens of the place, they ensured that there was never a dull moment at the castle—but these moments continue to resonate through our own time.

As with the Tower of London, former military residents seem to remain. In 1915, and again in 1947, the six-foot-high glowing figure of a man was seen walking between the Leerdam and Oranje bastions, and leaning over the parapet to stare into Darling Street. Disembodied footsteps are also frequently heard in the same areas of the castle, leading some to think that it is the same being, whatever it is. Its nearness leads other researchers to believe that the occasional ringing of the castle bell by itself—an eighteenth-century instrument imported from the Netherlands and the oldest in the country—may be traced to a guard who hanged himself with its rope. Perhaps, they theorize, he is the one stalking the battlements.

Footsteps are also heard on the battlements between Leerdam and Buren bastions (in the latter place, lights switch on and off by themselves). After World War II a levitating human shape without legs was seen in the same spot. So many screams, strange voices, and footsteps are heard in the castle late at night that the guards call their period of patrol the "ghost shift." The explanation, they are convinced, lies in the bloody history of the castle and the restless spirits of those tortured there centuries ago. There are soldiers who would rather walk around the outside of the building than pass through the haunted archways in the early morning. Worst, seemingly, is the entrance to the *Donker Gat* ("dark hole") dungeon. Most prisoners were horribly treated there, unlike the Zulu King, Cetewayo, who was allowed to bring his entire harem with him into his cell. The screams of agony heard coming from within do not sound like those of a harem.

In 1952, during the Van Riebeeck Festival celebrating the tercentenary of South Africa's founding, a couple was allowed to spend the night in the castle. They awoke late at night, and saw a lance corporal waking up the soldiers. Asked what he was doing, the soldier said that bus drivers and conductors were rioting in the streets. But the next day, there was no mention of this event in the papers, nor did any of the staff know about it.

But members of viceregal courts past make their appearances as well, including the eighteenth-century Dutch governor, Pieter Gysbert van Noodt. An unpleasant character in life, he is also seen and heard, cursing a blue streak. In April of 1729, the choleric van Noodt sentenced seven soldiers to death for desertion, after illegally overturning the council's lighter punishment. It so happened that one of the soldiers was a theology student. He stood on the gallows, summoning the governor to the judgment seat of God. That same day His Excellency was found dead in his chair.

A far happier spirit is that of Lady Anne Barnard, who lived at the castle during the first British occupation of 1795 to 1799. Lady Anne was the wife of the colonial secretary, Sir Andrew Barnard. Since the governor, Lord Macartney, had left his wife in Britain, and decided to live elsewhere, the Barnards were left to preside over the social life of the colony—a task Her Ladyship, at least, reveled in. In her letters to Henry Dundas, the secretary of war, and in many journals and drawings, she left behind a thorough picture of the Cape Colony in her time. She also transformed the large hall of the Kat residence into a ballroom, a function it maintained until recently.

When balls were held in honor of important visitors, Lady Anne's transparent ghost would sometimes make an appearance, apparently enjoying herself quite as much as she did at such things when she was alive. More often, she is seen at her favorite bathing spot in the castle, the Dolphin Pool. There is a picture of peacocks in a garden hanging in Lady Anne's drawing room in the castle. It is claimed that anyone who moves it shall certainly die.

Another specter that haunts the castle is one of the seemingly infinite regiment of "Gray Ladies," without whom the reader may begin to think no haunted castle is complete. Wearing a long cloak of that color, this particular Gray Lady has a very sad face, and walks the castle by night.

She also puts in appearances at nearby Tuynhuys. Originally built in 1700 as the Dutch East India Company's Guest House, specifically to accommodate important visitors, it was later remodeled for use as the government house, somewhat like Viceregal Lodge in Phoenix Park came to replace Dublin Castle. Lord Charles Somerset, the highly unpopular governor who left office in 1827 (and was responsible for the "1820 Settlers" coming from Britain to the Eastern Cape, as well as a number of other improvements to the colony), added a magnificent staircase, fireplaces, and an exquisite ballroom to the building. Somerset was also responsible for renaming the guest house the Government House. The castle became completely military and penal in nature, while Government

House acted as viceregal headquarters for the Cape Colony, and then for the Union of South Africa.

Inhabiting both centers of British rule as she does, it is believed that the Gray Lady's mortal remains were a woman's skeleton dug up near one of the castle's old "sally gates." In 1947, King George VI, his consort Queen Elizabeth, and their daughters the Princesses Elizabeth (now the Queen) and Margaret arrived in Cape Town for a tour of their South African dominion. They stayed at Government House while in town, and that was where the future monarch celebrated her twenty-first birthday. While the royal family was in residence, the Gray Lady was seen by several people, including Princess Margaret. She has put in a number of appearances since then.

Another strange artifact in the building is a portrait of Lord Charles Somerset, which causes dogs to bristle and snarl. In 1961, the Union of South Africa became a republic, and the governor-general was replaced by a president. The name "Tuynhuys" was resurrected for the building. Although it may be seen from Government Avenue, the limited access available to the public during viceregal times has now been completely suspended. If you want to see the Gray Lady, you will have to look for her at the castle. But who knows? They say she frequents a tunnel that runs between the castle and Tuynhuys. Perhaps you can follow her, and see the presidential residence from the inside!

Castle of Good Hope
Darling & Castle Street
Cape Town, South Africa

Tel: +27 (0) 21 787 1249
Fax: +27 (0) 21 787 1089
http://www.castleofgoodhope.co.za/

In Our Own Bailiwick

The United States of America is a strange nation in many respects. We have certainly seen the influence of the Old World, and we know that Native Americans and African-Americans, although relatively small minorities, have had a distinct influence on American life out of all proportion to their numbers—both because of their actual contributions to the culture and because of the important hold the sad histories of the conquest of the one and enslavement of the other has on the American mental landscape.

Apart from race, another major difference between America and Europe is the sheer size of the former, with its rapid settlement of a near-empty landscape. This fact, oddly enough, has managed to make Americans both wider-thinking *and* more provincial than their cousins in the Old World. As one writer has observed, the real distinctions between Europe and the largest country it gave birth to are "race and space."

These differences also are marked in the world of weird lore. We too have our "black hounds," our witches, and our "wise men." As noticed, the French in Canada and the Germans in Pennsylvania have made their contributions in these areas. From the Caribbean we derive voodoo and Santeria. But it was the United States that first developed a religion called Spiritualism, based on the belief in hauntings, which picked up a lot of its ideas (Indian spirit guides and the like) from that other quintessentially American faith called Shakerism.

American ghosts, like their counterparts across the world, show up in a wide variety of places. One of the most well-documented hauntings continues to take place in a Toys "R" Us in Sunnyvale, California. Here, toys fall off shelves, strange noises are heard, and cold spots abound. (In one account, an infrared photo revealed a young man leaning against a counter with his hands in his pockets, while a normal photo taken at just the same moment showed no such person.) But what of the castles and palaces we have been exploring?

Palaces, of course, are generally thought to require a monarch, or at least, as we saw in the chapter on the Commonwealth, a viceroy. Certainly the continental United States encompassed one actual kingdom (Hawaii), thirteen British colonies, five Spanish, and one French (Louisiana). Each of the colonies contained one or more "palaces" in the viceregal sense, but most of these are now gone. The two best known (the Governor's Palace in Williamsburg, Virginia, and Tryon's Palace in New Bern, North Carolina) are reconstructions. The one surviving such palace we will be looking at boasts its last viceroy as one of its ghosts.

In our discussion of the United States, we will enlarge the definition of "palace" to include any official residence of the executive authority on the state or national level. This is the custom in the rest of the Americas, where such places are called *Palacio Nacional*, *Palacio de Gobierno*, and the like. This Hispanic tradition is continued in the Indian pueblos of the Southwest, where the tiniest residence of the chief executive of a tribe is still called the "Governor's Palace."

Using such a criterion, the best-known haunted palace in the United States is certainly the White House in Washington, D.C. Many dead presidents have been seen in that building, but its most famous ghost is probably Abraham Lincoln. He introduced an air of the uncanny into the place while still alive. He and his wife held séances in the East Room, and some of his worst decisions were suggested to him from beyond. Lincoln also had a prophetic dream before he was murdered in which he saw himself lying in state. Since his death, the Civil War president has appeared to a number of witnesses, including Her Majesty Queen Wilhelmina of the Netherlands when she was overnighting in the Lincoln bedroom.

Unfortunately, since one of the criteria for inclusion in this book is accessibility to the public, we must leave the White House and its many phantoms alone. Since the terrorist attacks of September 11, 2001, it has become a very difficult place to enter. So we shall let it pass. But fear not! Most of the residences of the state governors can be visited, and they represent a ghastly harvest, indeed.

But what of castles? In colonial days, at least in Maryland and New York, there were manors and manor lords. Furthermore, plantation owners and merchant princes throughout the British colonies, and rancheros in the Spanish, lived in lordly style and built palatial residences—palatial for the time and place, that is. Although untitled, they treasured their heraldry and aspired to be (and to be seen as) real aristocrats.

After the Civil War, these sorts of folk were eclipsed by the new families they married into, whose truly enormous fortunes were based primarily on banking and industry. From about 1865 to 1950 or so, such favored clans emulated the nobility of Europe and particularly Britain—into whose families they occasionally married, bringing cash in return for a title. Those who stayed home revolutionized elite living. The Ivy League schools were reinvented along the lines of Oxford and Cambridge, while secondary boarding schools were patterned after Eton. The American branch of Anglicanism, the Episcopal Church, began to function like an established religion—hence the commencement of the National Cathedral.

But most striking of all was the change in architecture. Churches and courthouses became monumental, as did mansions. Houses modeled after continental castles and châteaus began to spring up all over the country. These magnificent piles were filled with antiques both European and American, and full staffs— complete with livery—were hired to run them. Biltmore in North Carolina, Winterthur and Nemours in Delaware, and Stan Hywet Hall in Ohio are typical of the breed.

Just how do they stack up on the haunting side, however? Well, many have more than their share of ghosts, to be sure. Given the large number of European antiques furnishing these homes, some are believed to have received their ghosts with the *objets d'art*. Thus Stan Hywet's "Gray Lady" came with an eighteenth-century bedroom set from England. But the similarly bedecked Hammond Castle's many ghosts were produced by its checkered past, as related in *The Ghosts of Hammond Castle* by John Dandola. Of course, by all rights, the most famous American castle—William Randolph Hearst's San Simeon—ought to be haunted, given its history. But all the employees that this author could interview declared that they had never heard of a haunting there.

Now, we must look at the ghosts of the ruling class in this most democratic of nations.

A Ghost Shares the Wine

illiam Penn laid out plans for the city of Dover in 1683, and in 1717, it was incorporated by the Delaware General Assembly. It became the capital of the state in 1777. After 1797—when his title was changed from president, as laid down in the 1776 state constitution—the governor presided over the town's political and social life. But it has only been since 1965 that the state's chief executives have resided in the old mansion called Woodburn. Nevertheless, the building's history goes back to the eighteenth century. In 1684, the land on which Woodburn is located was part of 412 acres given to one David Morgan. Although we cannot be sure, it seems that Morgan's family named the property Woodburn.

On November 2, 1784, Sheriff John Clayton sold the current tract to Charles Hillyard III. Hillyard came from a family that had held land grants in Delaware as early as the 1680s. Charles Hillyard's great-grandfather, John, had come to Kent County, receiving a land grant of about two thousand acres. After buying the Woodburn property, Charles built the house around 1798. As befitted his background, he erected a palace built in the middle Georgian period style. Featuring three full floors, an attic, and a cellar, Woodburn boasts brickwork laid in a Flemish bond design. Most notable of the rooms open to the public are the entrance hall, the drawing room, and the dining room, all enhanced by fine middle Georgian woodwork in such things as paneling, molding, and rails.

The enormous mansion was immediately filled. Hillyard and his wife Mary had ten children between the years of 1782 and 1798. At age fifty-four, he died in his home on January 25, 1814, predeceased by his wife. Their daughter Mary, together with her husband, Martin W. Bates, bought the place upon Charles's death, and lived on in the home for the next eleven years. A self-made man, Bates later became a U.S. senator.

On August 4, 1825, Daniel Cowgill Sr. bought Woodburn from Martin Bates for three thousand dollars. Cowgill was a newlywed, having married Mary Naudain just before moving into the house. Cowgill and his family became increasingly involved in the abolitionist movement, and during the 1840s and 1850s, the house served as a station on the Underground Railroad. It is said that a tunnel ran from a secret room in the basement underneath the rear grounds of the property out to the St. Jones River. From there, escaped slaves snuck into boats, traveling first from the St. Jones River, and then north along the Delaware River to the neighboring free states. In Delaware, itself a slave state, this was a perilous trade indeed.

On September 15, 1877, Edward H. Wilson married Coralee Cowgill, granddaughter of Daniel (and daughter of Daniel's son Clayton), in the house's great hall. Later, Woodburn was transferred to them and to Harriet Louise (Cowgill) Haman by Daniel Sr. and Clayton. A number of notable owners followed in quick succession. In 1912, U.S. Senator Daniel O. Hastings bought it.

The senator used the place primarily as a summer home, and made several improvements. He added a brick porch on three sides of the house, pillars on the south side, a French doorway in the drawing room, a reflecting pool in the garden, and removed the fireplace from the great hall. He sold Woodburn on September 12, 1918, to Mr. and Mrs. Frank Hall.

They in their turn also made a number of changes to Woodburn, but the high cost of maintaining the house forced the Halls to move to Bellevue Stratford in Philadelphia after World War II. After his wife died in 1952, Mr. Hall auctioned off the contents of the home, and then sold the house and one and a half acres of land. The remaining land was sold to the Elizabeth Murphy School.

The last private owners, the Murray family, sold the house to the state in 1965, for use as the governor's mansion. Delaware's chief executives have lived there ever since, and the house has become the venue for many official functions.

The first governor to live there from 1965 to 1969 was Charles L. Terry Jr., who gave leave to his wife to outfit Woodburn as a proper official residence, and opened it to the public for tours. They also began the tradition of holding an open house during the Christmas season.

Governor Sherman W. Tribbitt and his family were the first to use the house as their primary residence in the 1970s. Mrs. Tribbitt also began such customs at the house as exchange student tours, the Delaware Mother of the Year Tea, and press breakfasts. They also initiated the custom of planting a tree on the grounds each year. While governor from 1977 to 1985, Pierre S. du Pont IV, his wife, and their four children started hosting a Halloween celebration. Woodburn and its grounds were transformed into a haunted house for the amusement of guests. But in actuality, it had already been one for quite some time.

Around 1815, the Bates family was host to Lorenzo Dow, the famous Methodist missionary. At breakfast one morning, Mrs.

Bates asked the preacher to say grace. He asked if they shouldn't wait for the other houseguest. Surprised, his hostess told him that there were no other guests. Dow then described in some detail the older gentleman in powdered wig, knee britches, and ruffled shirt he had encountered on the staircase. Mrs. Bates was rather upset—Dow had described Charles Hillyard, her father and the builder of Woodburn, who had died the previous year.

Whether or not Mr. Hillyard returned again during his daughter's tenancy, he has come back since. In the 1870s, another houseguest had a fainting spell after seeing him sitting by the fireplace. Hillyard was renowned for his love of wine, which seems to continue beyond the grave. Governor Charles Terry Jr. blamed the ghost for draining off some of his vintage wines in the mansion's cellar. One of his servants saw the ghost drink from a decanter in the dining room. Earlier residents would often set out wine decanters containing more mediocre wines (which were drained overnight) in hopes of preserving their own higher-quality bottles. Frank Hall also saw the ghost many times on the stairway during his own long tenure. Inspired by Hall's example, Governor Tribbitt's wife, Jeanne, would regularly check the stairway for Hillyard's apparition, and also left wine out for him on numerous occasions. But apparently he has no truck with those looking for him. None of those attempts ever brought any results.

Another revenant is a small girl in a red-checked gingham dress and bonnet. Carrying a candle and walking on the grounds around the reflecting pool (which was added to the property by Senator Hastings), she must be of twentieth-century vintage. First seen playing by the pool during the 1940s, she has never been identified. When Governor Michael Castle held his inauguration party in January 1985, his guests complained that an invisible presence pulled at their clothing. One woman saw an apparition of a little girl in a corner of the reception room. Could it have been the girl from the reflecting pool?

Out on the south lawn near King's Highway, close to the south porch, is a large old tree with a huge hole in its trunk. Screams are heard emanating from it, often at Halloween, and at times the figure of a man hanging from two branches of the tree is seen. Moaning and the rattling of chains sometimes emanates from the basement as well, and popular legend suggests two opposite origins for these phenomena, which said legend also claims to be linked.

Both stories go back to the days of the Underground Railroad, when the Cowgills held sway. According to the first tale, a slave fleeing pursuit was caught hiding in the tree trunk's hole. The screams are supposed to be his. The chain rattling in the basement is said to be either his or that of another slave who was captured and sold. The alternative story is that the ghost who haunts the tree was actually a slave kidnapper, who had climbed the tree in hopes of finding runaways sponsored by Cowgill. Instead, he slipped, and his head was caught between two branches. Thus, according to some, he is presumed to be the hanging apparition, as well as the source of the strange noises in the basement.

The living, and official, tenants of Woodburn have tried to solve the mansion's mysteries. Undaunted by her lack of success with Charles Hillyard, Jeanne Tribbitt sought to confirm the presence of the other ghosts who share the house and grounds with Hillyard, but to no avail. Governor du Pont allowed college students to investigate the premises, but they came up with little evidence. Since a ghost crashed his inauguration party, it is no wonder that Governor Castle reported a few ghostly encounters himself. He permitted a teacher and three of her students, equipped with tape recorders and Ouija boards, to spend the night at Woodburn. In the morning they were all quite frightened, insisting that a portrait of a woman in one of the rooms had changed its expression, and had smiled at them all night.

Tours of Woodburn are open to the public Monday through Friday, 8:30 A.M. to 4:00 P.M., by appointment only. Will you be able to learn more than the current staff? Who knows. . . but should you encounter Woodburn's builder, see if he will share his wine.

The Governor's Mansion (Woodburn)
151 King's Highway
Dover, Delaware 19901

Tel: (302) 739–5656
http://www.state.de.us/capitolpd/governor.htm

Royal Phantom

A lthough many of the original states were colonies, and retain various relics of royal rule, only Hawaii boasts an actual royal palace. This is because the state had its own kings, from the time that Kamehameha I united the islands in the eighteenth century to the day Queen Liliuokalani was overthrown by American settlers in 1893.

Although the islands have been primarily Christian since the mid-nineteenth century, a great deal of native Polynesian supernatural lore survives. Even certain streets are said to be haunted, although few if any *haoles* (whites) have seen the spectral columns of "marchers" said to parade in plain sight.

The kings of Hawaii tried to reconcile modern European and American traditions with their own customs. One of these efforts at modernization was to turn the native kingship into a contemporary monarchy. This required a palace. The first one, built of wood, succumbed to the ravages of damp and termites. At last, King

David Kalakaua resolved to build one in stone. After demolishing the former residence, the king laid the cornerstone of a new palace on the last day of 1879. Completed and furnished by 1882, Iolani Palace cost the kingdom of Hawaii just under $360,000. It was the official residence of King Kalakaua from 1882 until his death in 1891, and of his sister and successor, Queen Liliuokalani, until her overthrow in 1893.

Sumptuously furnished, it hosted the coronation of King Kalakaua and Queen Kapiolani in 1883, as well as the king's fiftieth birthday celebration. But after her brother's death, the new queen's position became increasingly threatened by the American settlers. Although the rooms she nervously walked through boasted gifts from French, British, Russian, and German monarchs, no help was forthcoming. Not only was the queen at last deposed, she was tried and found guilty of treason against the republic which unseated her. For a short time she was under house arrest, until moving into her husband's family home at Washington Place.

From 1893 to 1968, Iolani Palace served successively as the capitol of the republic, the territory, and finally the state of Hawaii. When the new state capitol was completed in 1969, the palace was vacated and restored to its former splendor as a museum. The grounds have also been restored, and the Royal Hawaiian Band plays at times in the Coronation Pavilion.

But it would be strange, indeed, if the often tragic history of the palace had not left its mark upon the place. Often, when visitors have left, security guards will see unexplained lights and shadows, and hear footsteps when no one else is present. At times, wet footprints will appear in the halls—said to be left by a Hawaiian prince who was dunked in water as a punishment, and died of pneumonia. They say he still seeks his family.

Nor is the strangeness confined to the palace itself. Folks enjoying the gardens will smell odd scents, and hear unseen guards walking their rounds, invisible keys jingling as they walk. Unable to maintain their queen's authority in life, they still try to do so in death.

Most haunted of all is a disused, round, concrete fountain with stairs going underground. King Kalakaua had the palace well dug here for emergency use. Shortly after their victory over the monarchy, about a century ago, the triumphant republicans erected a decorative fountain which has since decayed due to neglect. Near this symbol of Hawaiian defeat, a glowing phantom girl in a white dress is sometimes seen. At sunset, she emerges from the locked doorway beneath the fountain, ascends eight stairs to the ground level, and floats about the palace exterior. She cries out to passersby, attempting to lure them to their doom—so far, unsuccessfully.

One shade is missing from Iolani Palace, however: Queen Lili-uokalani herself. But the wronged sovereign has been spotted elsewhere, both at the new state capitol (where she apparently objects to the placement of her statue in an obscure spot), at the Bishop Museum, and at Washington Place, now the Governor's Mansion, where she spent her last years in exile. But fear not. At her palace you may still encounter some of her loyal entourage.

Iolani Palace
364 South King Street
Honolulu, Hawaii 96804

Tel: (808) 538–1471
http://www.iolanipalace.org/
E-mail: miuraa@hawaii.edu

The Ghost Was a Gift

arson City was founded as a community in 1858. Pioneer Abraham Curry set aside ten acres expressly for the construction of a capitol, three years before the formation of the Nevada Territory. His prediction paid off: Carson City was designated both the territorial capital and the county seat of the newly formed Ormsby County. Three years later, Carson City was chosen state capital at the constitutional convention and remains so today.

Although the capitol was soon built, both territorial and state governors lacked a permanent residence. For over four decades, they lived wherever they could find a place. Finally, in 1907, State Assembly Bill 10, the "Mansion Bill," was passed to secure a permanent site for an official gubernatorial residence. Mrs. T. B. Rickey sold the land to the state for ten dollars. The classical revival building, with Georgian and Jeffersonian motifs, was designed by Reno architect George A. Ferris. The mansion was first occupied in July 1909 by acting governor Denver Dickerson and his family, and opened to the public for its first open house on New Year's Day, 1910. The governor's daughter, June Dickerson, was born in the mansion in September 1909, the only infant ever to be born there. Stairs and metal balustrades were added in 1969, and new buildings were constructed on the grounds in 1998.

As with any executive mansion in the United States, the Nevada governor's mansion has seen many dramatic episodes—the sort which often spawns ghosts. But for the most part, it has been a tranquil place, unaffected by the excitement which buffets such latter-day centers of mayhem in the state as Las Vegas, Reno, and the former Mustang Ranch. The mansion seemed to have escaped paranormal activity, and probably would have continued its placid existence, except for one rather small event, which occurred in what we like to think of as the halcyon days of the 1950s.

It was not a murder or suicide, a duel or thwarted love that started the ghostly ball rolling in the quiet governor's mansion. No, it was a gift: an otherwise unremarkable antique mantel clock. It seems that the inoffensive timepiece came complete with a ghost. The parlor doors began opening without any apparent help, and a cold, mobile "presence" began to be felt throughout the mansion. Eventually, a housekeeper saw a woman and her eight-year-old daughter—a ghostly pair, in fact—wandering through the rooms and hallways. No one knows who they are, or how they came to be associated with the clock.

Through most of the year, the mansion's living denizens and their staff are the only ones to confront the specters. But one day a year, you may have your chance. Fittingly, the ghostly date when the place is open for tours is Nevada Day, which is observed on the last Saturday in October. Sometimes the last Saturday falls on that spookiest of holidays, Halloween. That would probably be the best time to seek out the lady and her daughter.

But if you feel yourself safe from this particular haunting the other days of the year, bear in mind that what happened in the home of His Excellency of Nevada might happen to you. Be sure you know the history of every antique you acquire. You don't know what "added bonus" may come with it.

Nevada Governor's Mansion
606 Mountain Street
Carson City, Nevada 89706

Tel: (775) 882–2333
http://nv.gov/StateBldgs_Mansion.htm

Ben Franklin's Son Remains

Perth Amboy's history dates back to 1651. In that year, August Herman purchased the site of the town from the Lenni-Lenape Indians. Incorporated in 1683, settlers began to call the land Ambo or Amboy Point, and finally Amboy. When, three years later, the settlement became the capital of East Jersey, Perth was added to the name in honor of the Earl of Perth, one of the proprietors under the royal grant. In 1715, Perth Amboy received a royal charter from King George I.

As a result, Perth Amboy boasts the oldest city hall in continuous use in the United States. It was established in 1685 when the first courthouse was built. In 1713, a new structure was built on the same site. This later burned in 1731, and was rebuilt yet again about 1745. Still another fire claimed that building in 1764. At last, in 1767 the present city hall was built, containing court chambers, and rooms for the provincial assembly, the governor's council, and the city corporation.

The governor also needed a local residence, however. The proprietors of East Jersey built the Proprietary House between 1762 and 1764 for Governor Sir William Franklin. Designed by master architect John Edward Pryor, the Proprietary House was and is a grand Georgian-style house, truly fit for the king's representative. Of course, it was hard to lure Sir William away from his home in Burlington at Green Bank. This was not due to any overwhelming love for that town, but rather because it was only a few miles from Philadelphia, the governor's birthplace and continued residence of his celebrated (although illegitimate) father, Benjamin.

Although his mother's identity is unknown, William was raised by his father and Ben's maid, Deborah Read. He accompanied his father on several missions, including those to England, where he completed his education and was admitted to the bar. While there he met and courted Elizabeth Downes, a daughter of a wealthy Barbados sugar planter, and married her on September 4, 1762. They had one son, William Temple. Due to his father's popularity at court, when the Franklins returned from England in 1763, William carried a commission entitled His Majesty's Governor of New Jersey.

Initially, relations between father and son remained close, but they deteriorated over the years as rebellion loomed and Benjamin became ever closer to the rebels. By 1774, William's reluctance to leave Burlington had evaporated, and he looked at the spacious home built for him as a refuge. Refusing to break his oath to the king, the governor was grateful to have some space between his father and himself.

Trying to maintain the legal government in a province where the majority remained loyal but the wealthy and their militia favored rebellion, William Franklin found himself and his wife under house arrest at the Proprietary House in January 1776. The pressures upon him to both resign his commission and swear allegiance to the new regime daily mounted, as did the implied threats against his wife. He vowed that he would not leave the province.

Attempting to salvage the situation, in June he issued a proclamation as governor of New Jersey, summoning a meeting of the legal legislative assembly. But both he and his captors knew that a Loyalist majority would be returned to the Assembly. For this act he was arrested by order of the provincial congress of New Jersey, and removed to Burlington. His wife was left behind under continued arrest. Soon afterward he was sent to East Windsor, Connecticut. Elizabeth was subjected to continued harassment, until at last William Franklin's son, William Temple Franklin (who had allied with his grandfather), was able to obtain permission for her to pass through to British-occupied New York. Worn out by the treatment she had undergone during her imprisonment in her once luxurious home, she died without ever being reunited with her beloved husband.

William, in the meantime, remained strictly guarded in Connecticut, until, at last, in November 1778, he was exchanged for rebel prisoners and allowed to go to New York. Serving for a short time as president of the Board of Loyalists of New Jersey, he left for London in August of 1782. He died there in 1813.

His old house in Perth Amboy underwent many changes. After the Revolution, it became a private home. In 1809 it was transformed into a resort hotel, called the Brighton House, and in 1883 it was turned into a rooming home for retired Presbyterian ministers, called the Westminster. After that the grand old house became a flophouse. Fire, vandalism, vacancy, and depression all left their marks.

But new hope dawned for the Proprietary House in 1967, when the property was taken over by the state of New Jersey. Restoration and preservation measures were undertaken by the Proprietary House Association, which is an independent nonprofit organization made up of concerned local citizens. With minimal funding, the house is slowly regaining much of its former glory. Boasting a fine tearoom, it is open for visits. It also hosts a number of regular community events, including the annual re-creation of the arrest of Governor Franklin on June 9, 1776.

The tragic events of the Franklins' lives at the Proprietary House seem to have left a certain aftermath. Employees have seen a boy who appears to be pointing to the third floor, although no one claims to know why. It may have something to do, however, with an occurrence on that very floor. Two employees of the Verizon Company a few years ago went up there to repair some phones. There they met a lady in a white dress. When they asked her for some information as to the layout of the phone system, she vanished in front of their eyes. The pair fled downstairs, declaring to the staff that they would never set foot in the building again. Is it Elizabeth Downes Franklin, still guarding the grand home she was so proud of in life, despite the tragedy that overtook her there? Apparently this ghost tickles the cheeks of certain staff members, and claps her hands near their ears to signal her approval of their performance.

And what of her ill-starred husband? It is said by a former managing director that Sir William's influence can be felt most strongly around the anniversary of his arrest. This employee claimed to have seen—and heard—him on more than one occasion in her office on the ground floor.

Nor are these three the only spirits who appear to dwell in the house. What is one to make of the glowing orbs of light photographed in the tearoom and the servants' quarters? It's anyone's guess, of course, as to what or who they might be. What is certain is that the fare served in the tearoom is delicious, and the tour with its insight into a key story of our history is well worth attending. And who knows? Any expression of sympathy to the losers in that long-ago conflict might well bring some supernatural gratitude in return.

Proprietary House
149 Kearny Avenue
Perth Amboy, New Jersey 08861

Tel: (732) 826-5527
http://www.proprietaryhouse.org/
E-mail: info@proprietaryhouse.org

Ghosts Along the Mohawk

The Mohawk Valley of upstate New York is a fascinating place. There the Iroquois built their "castles," and there too the Johnson clan, headed first by Sir William and then by Sir John, carved out a feudal empire in the wilderness. Scots settlers came as tenants for the Johnsons, whose close connections to the Mohawks and political power in London made them a force to be reckoned with in the area. But all was lost as a result of the Revolution, when the rebels chased out the Johnsons' tenants in the middle of the winter of 1776. Although the latter returned repeatedly as Loyalist raiders, by 1783, it was all over. Loyalists and Mohawks alike had to remove to Canada.

But there would be at least one more castle built in the area, thanks to one John Beardslee, who arrived in 1781 from Connecticut in search of fortune. He found it, and, as a result, his son and heir, Augustus, was wealthy enough to begin construction of Beardslee Castle in 1860. As a politician and friend of President

Lincoln's, Augustus doubtless would have been ennobled had the American president had that kind of power. In any case, in building the family home he and his architects were inspired by Irish castles.

The next in line, Guy Beardslee, continued adding to the castle and the family fortune alike, pioneering in the sale of electricity. The castle benefited from this business, being electrified in 1898, when the Beardslee Power Company turned on the first lights in nearby St. Johnsville. But while the family was vacationing in Florida, eight years after selling the company in 1911, arson struck the castle. The building was completely gutted, leaving only the stone walls. Only the main floor would be rebuilt. The second floor was purposely left without a roof to save expense, and the back of the building was turned into a garden with stone walls draped in flowers and vines. Nevertheless, the Beardslees continued to live in both New York and Florida. In 1937, Guy died, followed by Ethel in 1941. There were no children.

Ethel left the castle to her sister. She in turn sold it in 1939 to one Anton "Pop" Christensen of St. Johnsville. He opened the estate to the public as "The Manor," allowing tours while he and his wife lived in a small cottage beside the castle in what is now the west courtyard. Having contracted a terminal illness, Pop eventually hanged himself in the ladies' room of the castle, in what is now the side entrance foyer.

Afterwards, the manor became a restaurant, falling in 1976 into the hands of Joe Casillo. Renaming the place Beardslee Manor, Casillo turned the basement into a pub in 1977, recovered the roof later, and finally added the second floor in 1982. In 1983, he brought in a professional ghost hunter. This worthy man spent the night and recorded disembodied voices on tape in front of re-porters. The ghosts became a draw until the place burned again in 1989. Abandoned, Beardslee Manor was a magnet for vandals until 1994. New people bought it, and renaming it Beardslee Castle, went out of their way to completely refurbish it. They have done a tremendous job in restoring the castle to its pre-1919 splendor. Parquet floors, paneled walls and ceilings, and Gothic arches reflect the wealth and romanticism of the Beardslees.

The building evokes the idea of a European haunted castle, a reflection of the reality within its walls. Even the road outside the castle is beset by phantoms. Back in the early 1950s, travelers along Route 5 would see a bright yellow or blue light. It most commonly rushed out at their cars from the woods, or else chased them down the road. The light was reported as blinding at times, and at others, it was seen floating off in the distance. As a result, several fatal accidents occurred at the bend in the road where the light was most often reported.

One woman said that the light rushed out from the trees and blinded her husband, who was at the wheel and subsequently died in the ensuing crash. Motorists have also seen a young child walking along the road late at night. Since 1996, there have been four cars that have driven off the road in the straight stretch in front of the castle. Just recently a couple was driving past the castle when a young lady stepped out into the road in front of them. Both the couple and the occupants of a car coming from the opposite direction were sure that the first car had plowed into the woman. But neither car's drivers or passengers, nor the police when they arrived, could find any trace of her. Nor were there any marks on the first automobile. Needless to say, no one was ever reported missing in connection with the incident.

The gardens too have their own phantoms. Guy Beardslee has been seen walking the grounds holding a lantern with a blue light, although some have just seen the lantern. In either case, he is believed to be searching for a lost child who either drowned in a pond or was hit by a train. He is not the only specter walking the grounds, however. There is also a woman in white who is seen sitting, walking, or standing by a window. Locals call her Abigail, and believe that she was a bride who died the night before her wedding.

The interior of the castle itself is not immune to such goings-on. On one night, when a few staff members were playing with a Ouija board, the lights suddenly went out. One of the players was slugged in the chest by an invisible hand and driven across the room. Some mornings, when the first employees arrive, they find overturned tables and chairs. Physical manifestation is an important part of this haunting, given the amount of silverware flying around and bottles and glasses breaking without any assistance.

But it is in the auditory realm that the spirits of Beardslee Castle really come into their own, as might well be gathered by the tape recording that began their fame. Employees have reported disembodied and unintelligible voices floating all around them, or have heard their own names called, as if by someone right next to them—when they were alone! A scream or howl seeming to emanate all around them once drove three staff members right out the door. However, there are nicer sounds as well. Both instrumental music and singing have been heard coming from empty rooms on the second floor. There are of course the usual doors opening and closing by themselves, disembodied footsteps, and keys jingling.

The castle has also acquired quite a reputation for bizarre "ghost photos." Quite a number of pictures showing odd things have been taken by visitors and staff. Certainly a stay here would do much to put you in touch with the area's past—perhaps, quite literally!

Beardslee Castle
123 Old State Road
Little Falls, New York 13365

Tel: (315) 823–3000; (800) 487–5861
http://www.beardsleecastle.com/

Where Ghostly Fiction is Fact

In the cool, green reaches of coastal Washington stands an English castle called Thornewood. Named in honor of and built by one Chester Thorne, it is an enduring testament to his vision. Thorne was one of the founders of the port of Tacoma, and built the castle as a gift for his bride, Anna. Thornewood Castle also reveals Thorne's fascination with old English estates, as well as the skill of his chosen architect, Kirtland Kelsey Cutter.

The house is a remarkable combination of native and imported materials and furnishings. In a mixed Tudor and Gothic style, Thornewood is simply huge, containing fifty-four rooms, including twenty-eight bedrooms and twenty-two baths. The place was built between 1908 and 1911. Its imported brick, oak paneling, oak staircase, and medieval stained glass were brought by three ships around Cape Horn to the Pacific Northwest—representing an entire fifteenth-century manor house bought in England and dismantled to be used in the construction. In 1911 it cost about one million dollars to build. Today it would cost about thirty million dollars. In a word, Thornewood Castle is unique on either continent.

The Thornes were great entertainers in their day. In fact, Presidents William Howard Taft and Theodore Roosevelt both spent the night in what is now the presidential suite. Thus, it makes sense that after a nationwide search, ABC-TV selected Thornewood as the structural star of its film, *Stephen King's Rose Red*. In both that chilling television movie and its prequel, *The Diary of Ellen Rimbauer: My Life at Rose Red*, the castle was used as the eponymous home that had an unpleasant habit of consuming people and spitting them out, so to speak, as ghosts.

Recounts the current owner: "During the filming of *Rose Red*, the crew was in the ballroom and a lamp just goes on. Everyone looked at each other to see who turned the lamp on but no one had touched it. Lights have a habit of going on and off. I was giving a tour as part of a High Tea, and it was probably a group of thirty people with me, and as I looked around I saw an apparition."

All the phantoms at Thornewood are not fictional, however! The current owners, Deanna and Wayne Robinson, rent out six rooms for bed-and-breakfast activity. One of these is Anna Thorne's room. Many ladies—but particularly brides before their weddings—sometimes see Mrs. Thorne sitting in the window seat behind them as they gaze in the mirror. When they turn, there is no one there.

Chester is also present, apparently. He has been seen walking the halls and playing the piano. He is also held responsible for the breakage of innumerable lightbulbs and occasional glass in the place.

Some guests staying in the Grandview Suite will see a child playing by the water outside. Fearful for his safety, they may rush outside to warn him away, only to find no one there. Mrs. Robinson believes that this is the ghost of a little boy who died in the 1970s. Saddest of all, perhaps, is the Thornes' son-in-law, General

Cadwallader Corse. The Thornes' daughter, Anita, divorced him shortly after he accidentally shot himself (the wound was not fatal) in the gun closet. Although he didn't die at Thornewood, his ghost is occasionally seen within its walls.

Here is a castle where the distinction between fact and fiction blurs. But is that so very strange, in the world of the supernatural?

Thornewood Castle
Lakewood, Washington 98409

Tel: (253) 584–4393
Fax: (253) 584–4497
http://thornewoodcastle.com/
E-mail: thornewood@mindspring.com

Afterword

So now, at last, we have come to the end of our tour. We have covered a lot of ground, both in time and space. It is interesting, in a way, that our two subjects—royals and nobles on the one hand, and ghosts on the other—are both very much opposed to the spirit of the age in which we live. Democracy, so-called, opposes the one, and materialism, the other.

But whether or not ghosts really do walk the earth, we will always be fascinated with them. Death, the great mystery, awaits us all, no matter how we attempt to disguise that fact. As we age, many of those we may have discussed the question with will have died themselves, and so be in a position, presumably, to know the answers to the questions. It seems to this author that one of the objections we moderns have to death and ghosts is that they appear to care little for what we believe is important. Trends mean nothing to the dead, and neither does success. All the multitudes of things we consumers are regularly told are important are shown up as mere baubles that in a little while will mean nothing.

We also remain fascinated with royalty and aristocrats. Part of the reason is that, no matter what the royals do, they are a living link with history, and with the founding of the country they inhabit. Their importance, to paraphrase Charles Fenyvesi, comes from the time when the first hero slew the dragon of chaos to inaugurate the rule of law.

We resent them for any implication that they are somehow better than us. It is seen to be intolerable that anyone should have privileges because of the circumstances of their birth. As a result, we exult when their behavior is as bad, or worse, than the normal run of folk. Yet in our hearts we expect more of them, and are angered by any such breaches of propriety. Regardless of public opinion, they continue to stalk the stage, even if deposed or exiled.

In different ways, in a time when we are assured that science knows all and that reason will triumph, both our presumed "betters" and ghosts represent mystery—something we both need and fear, and never more than now. The palaces and castles that both the highborn and the restless dead inhabit are concrete representations of that mystery, and will never lose their hold over our imaginations, regardless of history's turns and twists. Doubtless it is better so. A world without mystery hardly seems worth living in.

Charles A. Coulombe
Arcadia, California
Michaelmas 2004